Intrepid Explorers written by: Keith Lye
Illustrated by: Harry Bishop
Cover illustrated by: Harry Bishop

Race for the Moon written by: Robin Kerrod
Illustrated by: Jeff Burn, Roger Full Associates, Tony Gibbons,
            John Harwood, John Kelly

Designed by: Tri-Art
Series Editor: Christopher Tunney
Art Director: Keith Groom

Published by Christensen Press Limited, The Grange,
Grange Yard, London SE1 3AG.
© Christensen Press Limited 1985

First published 1985
Revised edition 1990

Printed and bound by Graficas Reunidas, Madrid, Spain.

ISBN: 0 946994 08 0

THE INTREPID Explorers

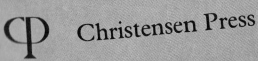 Christensen Press

What led to the great voyages of discovery in the Middle Ages?

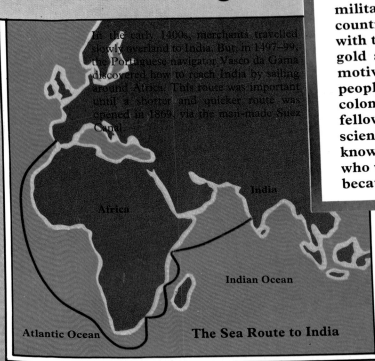

In the early 1400s, merchants travelled slowly overland to India. But, in 1497–99, the Portuguese navigator Vasco da Gama discovered how to reach India by sailing around Africa. This route was important until a shorter and quicker route was opened in 1869, via the man-made Suez Canal.

Africa

India

Indian Ocean

Atlantic Ocean

The Sea Route to India

WHY PEOPLE EXPLORE Since ancient times people have made journeys of exploration to find out more about the world. Though most of the world is now mapped, exploration still continues today. Many early explorers wanted to find new lands where they could trade. Others sought short cuts to far-away lands where they were already trading. Some explorers were military leaders. They conquered distant countries and brought back much information with them. Others hunted for treasure, such as gold and jewels. Missionaries had a different motive for travel. They wanted to convert people to their religion. Some explorers were colonizers. They looked for areas in which their fellow-countrymen could live. Others were scientists who wanted to increase Man's knowledge of the world. And there were many who went on journeys into the unknown simply because they loved adventure.

Did earlier peoples have the urge to explore?

The Macedonian king Alexander the Great led a Greek army against Persia. He defeated King Darius III at the Battle of Issus (near the Syrian–Turkish border) in 333 BC. Alexander marched to Egypt and then to India. He took scholars with him, and sent back reports about the conquered lands.

What reason is there for adventure today?

On May 29, 1953, the New Zealander Edmund Hillary and Sherpa Tensing Norgay became the first people to reach the top of the world—the peak of Mount Everest. This peak is 8,848 metres (29,028 feet) above sea level. Exploration of mountains is dangerous. It is usually undertaken by people who love adventure and enjoy testing their skill and endurance.

Does anyone explore for scientific reasons?

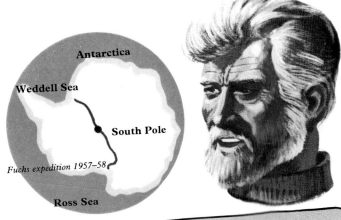

In 1957–58, Sir Vivian Fuchs, a British scientific explorer, led the first expedition across Antarctica, via the South Pole. Fuchs, a geologist, made scientific observations throughout his 99-day journey.

Why did Norsemen go to North America?

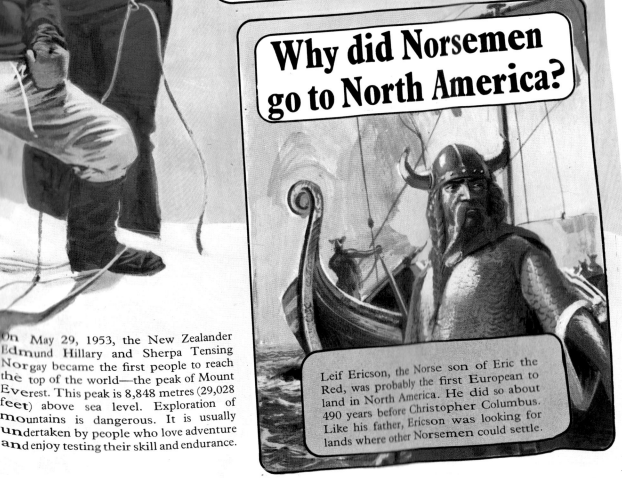

Leif Ericson, the Norse son of Eric the Red, was probably the first European to land in North America. He did so about 490 years before Christopher Columbus. Like his father, Ericson was looking for lands where other Norsemen could settle.

EARLY EXPLORERS included Egyptian, Phoenician, and Carthaginian traders. The Greeks, too, made many journeys of exploration. They realized that the Earth was round, and they developed the foundations of modern map-making. A Greek scholar, Ptolemy, summarized Greek knowledge of the world in the AD 100s. The ancient Romans were great soldiers and law-makers, but they added little to Greek knowledge of geography. In the 1,000 years after the decline of the Roman empire, there were few European explorers, apart from Marco Polo. Most people feared the unknown.

Were there any great navigators in the ancient world?

What did long-distance Greek ships look like?

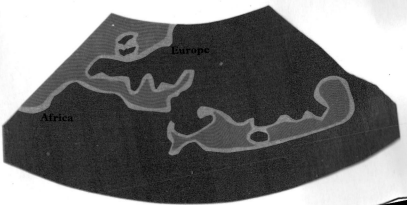

Iceland

British Isles

Atlantic
Ocean

Spain

The route probably taken by the Greek explorer Pytheas in about 325 BC. Many people did not believe his stories, especially of the frozen ocean which he claimed he saw in the far north.

Greek ships, called triremes, were large and sturdy and were probably like the one shown here. The Greeks may have used them for long journeys of exploration. Each trireme had about 170 oarsmen, arranged in three rows. Some triremes were 45 metres (150 feet) long.

What was known about the world in ancient times?

In his book *Geography*, Ptolemy summarized Greek knowledge of the world in the AD 100s. One of his chief mistakes was his belief that the world was smaller than it really is.

Europe

Africa

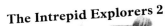

Were medieval Asians and Europeans in contact?

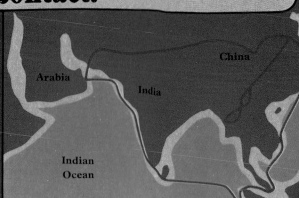

Right: Marco Polo dressed in Mongolian clothes. Between 1271 and 1275, Marco Polo, a Venetian, travelled with his father Nicolò and his uncle Maffeo, two merchants, across central Asia to China (see map, *left*). In China, they stayed at the court of the emperor Kublai Khan. Marco Polo explored many parts of China. Between 1292 and 1295, the Polos journeyed home, mostly by sea.

What ideas did Europeans have about unknown lands?

Fear of the unknown led many people to imagine that the world beyond the known areas was full of strange monsters. They thought that there were weird, ferocious beasts, and men with the heads of animals. Some of these frightening creatures were shown in Marco Polo's book describing his travels in Asia.

FINDING THEIR WAY In ancient times, ships usually sailed within sight of land so that sailors could find their position from landmarks. But when storms blew ships off course, the sailors lost their way. Astronomy finally came to the aid of navigators. Astronomers found that, as the Earth rotates, the stars in the sky appear to move around. But one star, the Pole Star, stays roughly in the same place. The reason is that the Pole Star is almost directly overhead at the North Pole, one end of the Earth's axis. Astronomers realized that the angle of the Pole Star above the horizon was roughly the same as the latitude (north-south position) of a navigator. Measuring longitude (east-west position) was not easy until the invention of the chronometer, an extremely accurate clock, in the 1700s.

What is latitude?

Latitude is measured from the equator (0° latitude) to the North Pole (90° North) and the South Pole (90° South). The latitude of any place is the angle at the centre of the Earth formed between the equator and the place.

Why was the Pole Star important to navigators?

How did explorers measure the angle of the Pole Star?

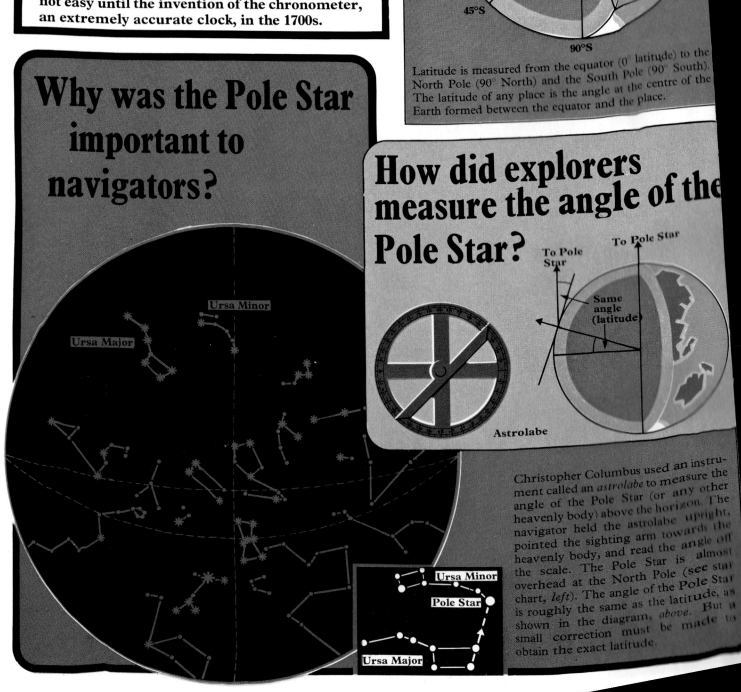

Astrolabe

Christopher Columbus used an instrument called an *astrolabe* to measure the angle of the Pole Star (or any other heavenly body) above the horizon. The navigator held the astrolabe upright, pointed the sighting arm towards the heavenly body, and read the angle off the scale. The Pole Star is almost overhead at the North Pole (see star chart, *left*). The angle of the Pole Star is roughly the same as the latitude, as shown in the diagram, *above*. But a small correction must be made to obtain the exact latitude.

What is longitude?

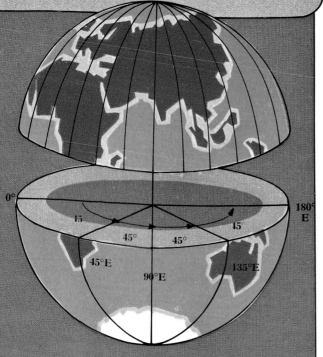

Longitude is measured east and west of the *prime meridian*, the line of longitude that passes through the North and South Poles and Greenwich, in London. On the equator, the longitude of any place is the angle formed at the centre of the Earth between the prime meridian (0° longitude) and the place.

How is longitude measured today?

With a chronometer, an accurate clock, navigators work out their longitude. They compare the time at Greenwich (on the chronometer) with local time, measured from the position of the Sun in the sky. One hour difference equals 15° of longitude.

Sand glass

How did early navigators find longitude without chronometers?

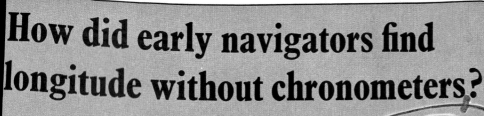

Before the chronometer was invented, navigators used a method called *dead reckoning*. They found the direction in which they were sailing by taking a compass bearing. They worked out the ship's speed by using a sand glass to measure the time it took to cast out a log chip and line (a rope with a weight on the end). Along the line were pieces of cloth every 14.4 metres (47 feet 4 inches). Knowing the ship's speed, they then worked out how far they sailed in any direction, and marked their position on a map.

Log chip and line

Compass

Who was the most famous 'navigator' of the 1400s?

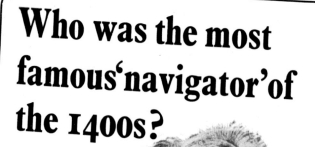

Henry the Navigator was the third son of the King of Portugal. A man of great learning, Prince Henry encouraged the exploration of the west coast of Africa. But although he was called 'the Navigator', Prince Henry himself never went on any of the expeditions of discovery.

A SEA ROUTE TO THE EAST Europeans became interested in exploration again in the 1400s, when the great Age of Discovery began. Their interest was partly due to their need to trade. Scholars studied Ptolemy's book 'Geography', which had been preserved by the Arabs. Prince Henry, the son of the King of Portugal, played an extremely important part in encouraging navigation. Prince Henry set up a school of navigation, where his engineers designed new ships that were better fitted for long ocean journeys. He sponsored the exploration of the coast of Africa, and this work continued after his death in 1460. Vasco da Gama discovered the sea route to India in 1498.

Henry the Navigator's school of navigation was at Sagres, in south-western Portugal.

Portugal

Spain

Sagres

Mediterranean Sea

Atlantic Ocean

Africa

What kind of ship is associated with him?

The caravel was an ocean-going ship developed by the Portuguese and Spaniards in the 1400s. Prince Henry the Navigator encouraged the development of caravels, which were used in exploration. They had two main types of sails. The square sails were used for moving fast when there was a strong wind behind the ship. The triangular 'lateen' sails made use of light or side winds. The ships were small, but they had room for supplies of water and food.

Who was the first explorer to round the Cape of Good Hope?

Africa

Indian Ocean

Dias 1487

Cape of Good Hope

In 1487, the Portuguese Bartolomeu Dias, *right*, sailed around the Cape of Good Hope, at the southern tip of Africa. He was the first European to do so in the Age of Discovery. But Phoenicians may have sailed around Africa in about 600 BC.

Why was Vasco da Gama's voyage such a triumph?

Europe

Africa

India

Vasco da Gama 1497–99

After 1453, the Turks had blocked the traditional land routes from Europe to India. But Europeans wanted silks, spices, and other luxuries. For this reason, they thought Vasco da Gama's voyage of discovery around Africa in 1497–99 very important.

Did medieval exploration help Africa?

The Portuguese explorers who charted the coast of Africa were followed by traders. The African coastlands were not rich, although they had some gold and ivory. But there was another valuable item—human beings who could be captured as slaves. Traders mostly bought slaves from coastal African chiefs who raided inland villages. Soon Britain, France, Holland, and Spain also traded in slaves.

Vasco da Gama

WESTWARD HO! Christopher Columbus led perhaps the best-known journey of exploration when, in 1492, he sailed across the Atlantic Ocean. After 10 weeks at sea, he landed on San Salvador, in the Bahamas. He also visited Hispaniola (now Haiti and the Dominican Republic) and Cuba. In 1493, 1498, and 1502, he again explored the West Indies, and sighted South America, which he believed to be Asia.

What was Columbus's ship like?

Why did Columbus think he had reached Asia?

North America   Europe

Atlantic Ocean

The World As It Is

Europe

Asia

Atlantic Ocean

The World As Columbus Thought It Was

Columbus thought that the Earth was much smaller than it is. When he had sailed a certain distance, he calculated that he must have reached Asia.

In 1492, Columbus sailed with three caravels, the *Santa María*, his flagship, *above*, and the smaller *Niña* and *Pinta*. The *Santa María* was about 35 metres (115 feet) long and had a crew of 40. It was wrecked on Hispaniola and Columbus returned home with the *Niña* and the *Pinta*.

Why were his sailors frightened by sailing long distances?

What routes did he follow?

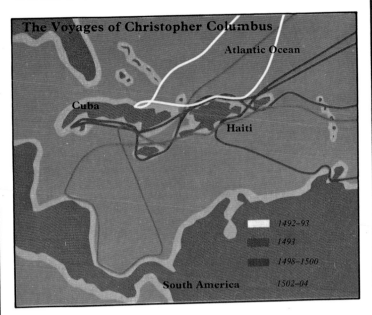

The Voyages of Christopher Columbus

Atlantic Ocean

Cuba

Haiti

South America

	1492–93
	1493
	1498–1500
	1502–04

Columbus's first voyage took him to the Bahamas, Hispaniola, and Cuba. On his later voyages, he discovered Dominica, Guadeloupe, and Trinidad. During his third voyage (1498–1500), he became the first European to sight South America, but he did not understand its significance.

In the 1400s, many sailors feared long ocean journeys. Some thought that terrible serpents would devour them in the open sea. Others thought that they might fall off the edge of the Earth.

Who were his patrons?

On Columbus's triumphant return to Spain in 1493, King Ferdinand and Queen Isabella confirmed his title 'Admiral of the Ocean Sea'. They also gave him the title 'Viceroy of the Indies', in the mistaken belief that he had reached the Indies in Asia. Columbus was born in Genoa, Italy. He was a skilled navigator, and he wanted to find a patron for his expedition to sail westwards to Asia. He tried to win the support of the king of Portugal but failed. He finally managed to persuade Spain to help him.

How did Magellan reach the Pacific?

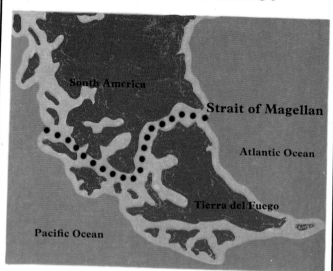

South America
Strait of Magellan
Atlantic Ocean
Tierra del Fuego
Pacific Ocean

The Strait of Magellan is a narrow, dangerous waterway, linking the Atlantic and Pacific oceans. It runs between the southern tip of the South American mainland and offshore islands. Magellan's ships entered the Strait in October 1520, and reached the Pacific in late November.

AROUND THE WORLD   A Portuguese, Ferdinand Magellan, achieved Columbus's aim of reaching Asia by sailing westwards. He set out from Spain in September 1519, and sailed down the coast of South America. In November 1520, he discovered the Strait of Magellan, leading into the Pacific Ocean. In April 1521, Magellan was killed in the Philippines, but one ship, under the command of Juan Sebastián del Cano, managed to complete the first round-the-world voyage. An Englishman, Sir Francis Drake, achieved the same feat in 1577-80.

What happened to Magellan?

Did explorers bring their religion and customs with them?

Ferdinand Magellan introduced his own religion—Christianity—into the Philippines, which he reached in March 1521 after a long, slow journey across the Pacific Ocean. Today, the Philippines remains the only Christian country in Asia.

In the Philippines, Magellan converted the ruler of the island of Cebu to Christianity. This ruler told Magellan of his enemies on the nearby island of Mactan. Magellan decided to attack Mactan, but he was killed there on April 27, 1521. The disappointed ruler of Cebu killed several of Magellan's officers.

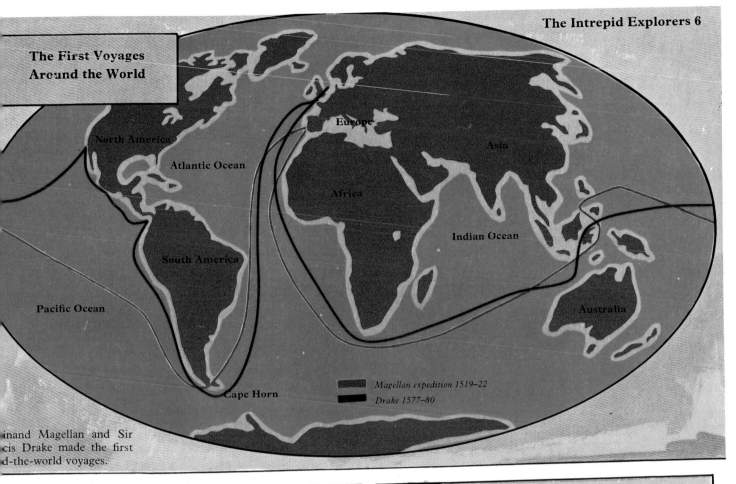

The First Voyages Around the World

North America
Atlantic Ocean
Europe
Asia
Africa
Indian Ocean
South America
Pacific Ocean
Cape Horn
Australia

▬ Magellan expedition 1519–22
▬ Drake 1577–80

...inand Magellan and Sir ...cis Drake made the first ...d-the-world voyages.

What was the second ship to sail around the world?

Sir Francis Drake's ship, first called *Pelican* and renamed *Golden Hind*, completed the second round-the-world voyage. The ship carried 18 guns and various other weapons. It had to serve as a ship of war as well as a merchant ship. The *Golden Hind* was a small vessel of only about 100 tonnes, with a crew of about 80 men. But it carried food for 18 months and rich treasures plundered from Spanish ships.

Were the pioneers treated as heroes?

A few months after Drake's return from his round-the-world voyage, Queen Elizabeth I knighted him aboard the *Golden Hind*. Drake had brought back plundered treasures worth about £18 million today.

How did the Americas get their name?

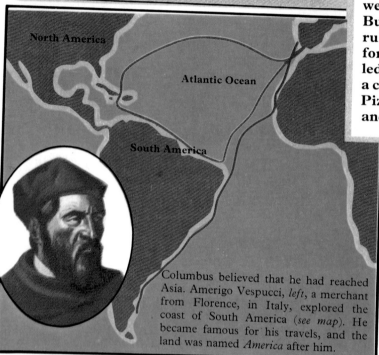

Columbus believed that he had reached Asia. Amerigo Vespucci, *left*, a merchant from Florence, in Italy, explored the coast of South America (*see map*). He became famous for his travels, and the land was named *America* after him.

THE SEARCH FOR TREASURE When people realized that Columbus had discovered a 'New World', many adventurers wanted to see what treasures they could find in it. In 1519, a Spaniard, Hernan Cortés, took a small armed force to Central America. The Aztecs, who had built up a great empire in what is now Mexico, at first welcomed Cortés. They thought he was a god. But Cortés captured Montezuma, the Aztec ruler, plundered his empire, and seized Mexico for Spain. Another Spaniard, Francisco Pizzaro, led an expedition in 1531 against the Inca empire, a civilization with its centre in what is now Peru. Pizzaro captured the Inca ruler, Atahualpa, and held him hostage before executing him.

Who was the first explorer to cross Central America?

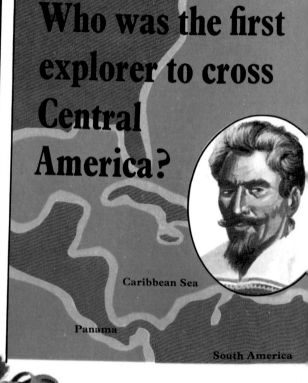

The narrowest part of the American continent is in what is now called *Panama*. In 1513, a Spaniard named Vasco Núñez de Balboa crossed Panama and became the first European to see the Pacific Ocean from the Americas. He called it *South Sea*. It was renamed by Ferdinand Magellan.

Why was Cortes so successful?

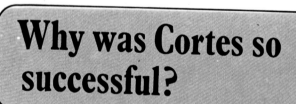

The Aztecs believed that a god named Quetzalcoatl would return to the country in 1519. Legends told of the god's white face and short beard. It was said that he would wear a high-crowned hat and carry strange weapons. When the Aztecs saw Cortés, they thought he was Quetzalcoatl.

What happened to the Incas?

Francisco Pizzaro, *top right*, was a Spanish adventurer who plundered the wealth of the Inca empire, in what is now Peru. He was looking especially for gold and silver. Inca craftsmen made these metals into beautiful ornaments, such as the golden toucan, *bottom right*. Pizzaro captured the Inca ruler Atahualpa in 1532. He then demanded that the people bring treasures to him as ransom. A vast treasure was given to him. But Pizzaro still had Atahualpa strangled.

Who first explored the Amazon?

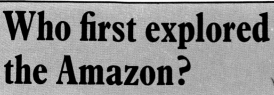

Route of Francisco de Orellana

South America

In 1541, the Spaniard Francisco de Orellana travelled into the lands around the Amazon River. With him was Francisco Pizzaro's brother Gonzalo. Orellana went ahead to look for food, but could not return because the river currents were too strong. Instead, he explored the river. He called it the *Amazon* because he saw armed women on the banks. In Greek legends, female warriors were called *Amazons*.

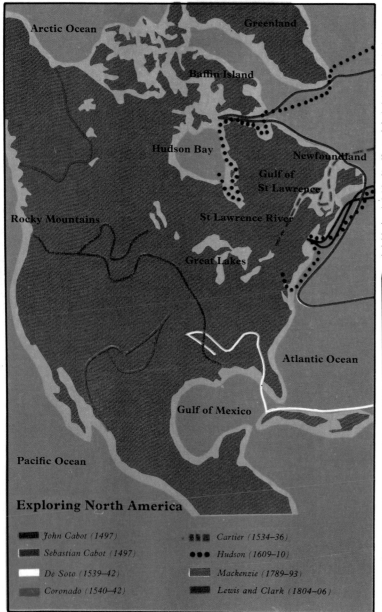

Arctic Ocean
Greenland
Baffin Island
Hudson Bay
Newfoundland
Gulf of St Lawrence
Rocky Mountains
St Lawrence River
Great Lakes
Atlantic Ocean
Gulf of Mexico
Pacific Ocean

Exploring North America

- John Cabot (1497)
- Sebastian Cabot (1497)
- De Soto (1539–42)
- Coronado (1540–42)
- Cartier (1534–36)
- Hudson (1609–10)
- Mackenzie (1789–93)
- Lewis and Clark (1804–06)

INTO AND AROUND NORTH AMERICA In 1497, John Cabot became the first European to reach the North American mainland since the Vikings, 500 years earlier. Like Columbus, he thought he was in Asia. Cabot's son Sebastian reached the entrance of what is now called Hudson Bay in 1509, and Henry Hudson explored the bay (named after him) on his ill-fated journey in 1610–11. Early explorers of the southern interior were Spanish treasure hunters and Frenchmen, such as Jacques Cartier. The first man to reach the Pacific coast of Canada by land was the Scot Alexander Mackenzie in 1793. And in 1804–06, Lewis and Clark explored the north-western United States, and reached the Pacific.

Did medieval Europeans explore the North American coast?

John Cabot

John Cabot was an Italian who led an English expedition from Bristol across the North Atlantic. He reached what are now Newfoundland and Nova Scotia in 1497. He was accompanied by his son Sebastian.

What kind of people did explorers find in North America?

The Spanish adventurer Hernando de Soto visits an Indian camp on the Mississippi River. The peoples of the Americas were called *Indians* because early explorers thought they had reached Asia. De Soto explored the south-eastern part of what is now the United States between 1539 and 1542. Earlier, he had been with Pizzaro in Peru.

Who first explored the St Lawrence?

On his first voyage to North America in 1534, the Frenchman Jacques Cartier erected a huge cross at Gaspé peninsula near the mouth of the St Lawrence River. He also made an expedition in 1535, and sailed about 1,300 km (800 miles) up the river.

Who discovered Hudson Bay?

On his second voyage of discovery in 1610, the Englishman Henry Hudson discovered the Hudson Strait and the vast Hudson Bay. But his crew mutinied. Hudson, his son John, and seven others were cast adrift in a small boat. They were never heard of again.

Who first crossed the United States?

Between 1804 and 1806, the American Meriwether Lewis and his second-in-command William Clark led the first expedition to cross the United States by land. They kept detailed records, and mapped their journey from St Louis, on the Mississippi River, to the estuary of the Columbia River, on the Pacific Coast. They made friendly contact with tribes of American Indians. Most of these were unknown before the expedition. The members of the expedition suffered great hardships, but only one man was lost during the long journey.

Who were the first explorers of Australia?

Exploring the Coasts of Australia and New Zealand

Timor Sea

Indian Ocean

Australia

Pacific Ocean

New Zealand

Key (map legend):
Jansz (1605–06)
Hartog (1616)
Tasman (1642–43)
Tasman (1644)
Cook (1768–71)
Flinders (1801–03)

The chief voyages of discovery around the coasts of Australia and New Zealand were made between 1600 and the early 1800s. The earliest pioneers of this exploration were Dutch sailors. They were followed by the British.

THE SOUTHERN CONTINENT

From early times, Europeans had believed that there must be a southern continent to 'balance' those in the north. The first known European landing in Australia was made in 1606 when a Dutchman, Willem Jansz, entered the Gulf of Carpentaria in the north. The Dutch later explored the northern and western coasts, and in 1642–43 Abel Tasman discovered Tasmania and New Zealand. In 1768–71, Captain Cook explored the coasts of New Zealand and the eastern coast of Australia. Then, in 1801–03, Matthew Flinders sailed right round Australia. The interior was explored in a series of daring and sometimes tragic journeys in the 1800s.

Why did the Dutch cease their exploration?

The Dutch explored the northern and western coasts of Australia. But these areas did not attract the Dutch sailors because they were mostly infertile and were populated by hostile Aborigines. An example of this hostility was the killing of several members of Willem Jansz's crew in the early 1600s.

Who first explored Australia's Pacific coast?

Captain Cook made three great voyages of discovery. In 1768–71, Cook explored the coasts of New Zealand and the eastern coast of Australia. There, he found fertile areas that afterwards became British settlements. Cook later explored the Antarctic Ocean. His last voyage took him to the Pacific, where he was killed in Hawaii in 1779.

What was Captain Cook's ship like?

Captain Cook's ship *Endeavour* had formerly been used to carry coal from England to Scandinavia. Cook refitted the ship, and had new cabins built for the officers. The *Endeavour* was about 30 metres (100 feet) long. Its greatest width was about 9 metres (30 feet).

Who first crossed central Australia?

Exploring Australia

Among the epic journeys into the interior of Australia, one of the best known is that of Robert O'Hara Burke and William Wills. These men made the first overland journey across Australia from north to south. They travelled with camels from India. Burke and Wills both died on the return journey. Their companion, John King, was found starving in an Aborigine village.

Sturt (1829–30)
Sturt (1844–45)
Leichhardt (1844–45)
Burke and Wills (1860–61)
Stuart (1860–62)
Forrest (1874)

What were explorers looking for in Africa?

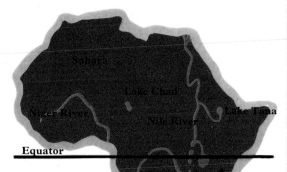

In the early 1800s, the main mysteries of African geography were the sources of the major rivers, including the Nile, Niger, Zambezi, and Congo (now called the Zaïre). The great lakes, from which some rivers flowed, were also sought.

INTO AFRICA The coasts of Africa were mapped during the great Age of Exploration in the 1400s and 1500s. But Africa remained the 'Dark Continent' until the 1800s, because Europeans seldom ventured far inland. From the 1500s, most of the Europeans who went to Africa south of the burning Sahara were slave traders. They bought slaves from coastal African chiefs. The mapping of the interior was largely undertaken by men who suffered great hardships to solve the mysteries of African geography. Mungo Park explored the Niger River, but died before his work was finished. John Hanning Speke realized that Lake Victoria was the source of the White Nile, but he could not prove it. David Livingstone explored the Zambezi and various lakes, and Henry Morton Stanley the Congo (now Zaïre) River. Some missionary explorers did much to stop the cruel slave trade.

What difficulties did they face?

Exploration of the interior of Africa was late for several reasons. In many areas south of the Sahara, the land rises steeply behind a narrow coastal plain. European ships could not navigate the rivers which tumbled down the steep slopes. The hot, forested coasts were disease-ridden, and there were many dangerous animals. Also, many Africans fought against outsiders.

Who said 'Dr Livingstone, I presume'?

Henry Morton Stanley, a newspaper reporter, *left, above,* found David Livingstone at Ujiji (now in Tanzania) on October 28, 1871. Livingstone had not been heard of for some time and Stanley greeted him with the famous words: 'Dr Livingstone, I presume.'

How did explorers travel about in Africa?

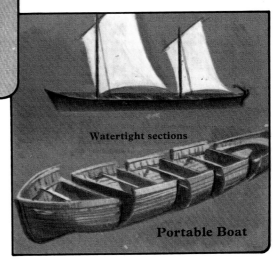

Watertight sections

Portable Boat

The missionary-explorer David Livingstone, *far left,* often rode on an ox. The German explorer Heinrich Barth, *left,* disguised himself as an Arab while exploring the Sahara. Henry Morton Stanley's boat, *above,* could be dismantled and carried when he met a waterfall on the Congo River.

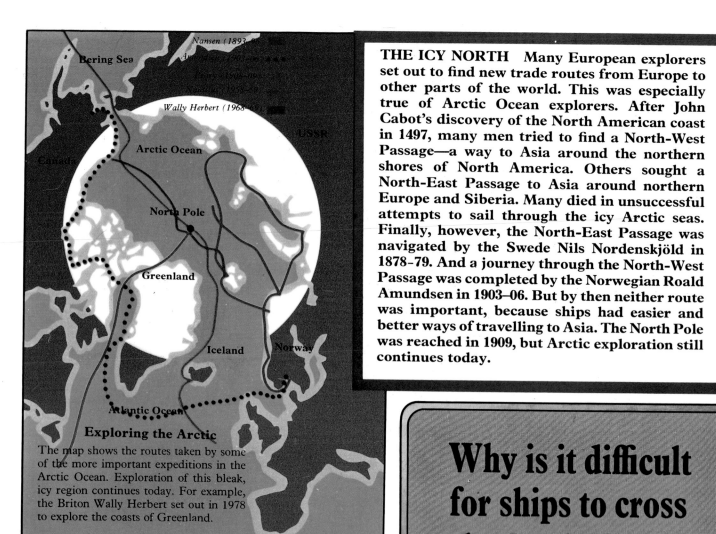

In the map (top left):

Nansen (1893–...)
...1903-0...
Peary (1908-09)
Nautilus (1958-59)
Wally Herbert (1968-...)

Bering Sea

Canada

Arctic Ocean

USSR

North Pole

Greenland

Iceland

Norway

Atlantic Ocean

Exploring the Arctic

The map shows the routes taken by some of the more important expeditions in the Arctic Ocean. Exploration of this bleak, icy region continues today. For example, the Briton Wally Herbert set out in 1978 to explore the coasts of Greenland.

THE ICY NORTH Many European explorers set out to find new trade routes from Europe to other parts of the world. This was especially true of Arctic Ocean explorers. After John Cabot's discovery of the North American coast in 1497, many men tried to find a North-West Passage—a way to Asia around the northern shores of North America. Others sought a North-East Passage to Asia around northern Europe and Siberia. Many died in unsuccessful attempts to sail through the icy Arctic seas. Finally, however, the North-East Passage was navigated by the Swede Nils Nordenskjöld in 1878-79. And a journey through the North-West Passage was completed by the Norwegian Roald Amundsen in 1903–06. But by then neither route was important, because ships had easier and better ways of travelling to Asia. The North Pole was reached in 1909, but Arctic exploration still continues today.

Why is it difficult for ships to cross the Arctic Ocean?

Ships have been trapped and crushed in the Arctic sea ice. But the sturdy *Fram*, used by the Norwegian Fridtjof Nansen, *above*, reached about latitude 84° North in the winter of 1894–95. Then, on foot, Nansen got within 438 km (272 miles) of the North Pole.

Who first reached the North Pole?

The American Robert Peary reached the North Pole on April 6, 1909. He was the first person to do so. Huskies drew his sledges over the ice.

Who first made a surface crossing of the Arctic?

The explorer Wally Herbert led the British Trans-Arctic Expedition of 1968–69 from Point Barrow in Alaska to Spitzbergen, via the North Pole.

Has anyone sailed 'under' the North Pole?

The *Nautilus*, the first nuclear-powered submarine, was built in the United States in 1955. In 1958, it sailed under the North Pole.

A POLAR CONTINENT The ice-covered continent of Antarctica was the last to be discovered. In 1773, Captain James Cook sailed across the Antarctic Circle, but turned back because of pack ice. In the early 1800s, seal and whale hunters sailed the southern seas. And, in 1819-21, the Russian Fabian von Bellingshausen sailed almost entirely around Antarctica. The first certain landing on the continent was in 1831. The race for the South Pole took place in 1911. The victor was the Norwegian Roald Amundsen, who beat the Briton Robert Falcon Scott by a month. In the 1950s, a new phase of scientific exploration began. A major achievement was the Trans-Arctic Expedition of 1957-58 led by Sir Vivian Fuchs.

Cook (1773-74)
Bellingshausen (1819-21)
Scott (1911-12)
Amundsen (1911)

Atlantic Ocean

Weddell Sea

South America

South Pole

Ross Sea

Pacific Ocean

Australia

Exploring Antarctica
The map shows some of the major voyages of discovery in the icy Antarctic Ocean, and the overland routes of Roald Amundsen and Robert Falcon Scott in their race for the South Pole in 1911. Amundsen returned in triumph, but Scott's team perished on their homeward journey in 1912.

What difficulties did explorers face in Antarctica?

How did Scott's expedition pull sledges?

Robert Falcon Scott wrote in his diary: 'Great God, this is an awful place!' Scott's team faced many hardships. Lack of fresh food led to scurvy, low temperatures caused frostbite, and the icy blizzards sapped their strength.

Scott took 19 sturdy Siberian ponies to draw his sledges. But the ponies, unlike Amundsen's dogs, could not withstand Antarctic conditions, and, one by one, they died. Then, Scott's men had to haul their own sledges, an exhausting task in Antarctica.

Who first reached the South Pole?

Leaving his ship, the *Fram*, anchored in the Bay of Whales, Roald Amundsen set out for the South Pole in October 1911. Siberian huskies were used to draw the light sledges. Amundsen and his four companions wore fur garments, which were light but warm. They travelled quickly. They reached the South Pole on December 14, 1911, and erected the Norwegian flag.

Has anyone flown over the Poles?

Richard E. Byrd, an American aviator and polar explorer, flew to the North Pole from Spitzbergen in 1926. In 1929, he flew to the South Pole. Byrd was the first person to achieve these feats. He later did much scientific research in Antarctica.

How would a modern Antarctic expedition travel?

The *Sno-cat* is a modern tracked vehicle with low gears, specially designed for travel in Antarctica. Some *Sno-cats* carry a crevasse detector ahead of them. They cross crevasses on light metal ramps, which are placed over the dangerous holes.

Have the ocean floors been mapped?

EXPLORING SEAS AND OCEANS

The oceans cover more than seven-tenths of the Earth's surface. But exploration of the ocean depths began only recently. Early navigators were interested in surface currents and tides, but no one could descend far beneath the waves, because of the tremendous pressure of the water. Before 1930, no one had gone down more than 180 metres (600 feet). The invention of the bathyscaph, a diving vessel, made possible the record descent of 10,917 metres (35,817 feet) in 1960. Scientists began to study the ocean bed in the 1800s, but it was a slow job. At first, depths were measured by dropping a weight attached to a line. After 1919, echo-sounders came into use, and speeded up ocean-floor mapping. Discoveries about the nature of the ocean bed have confirmed the theory that the continents were once joined together, but have drifted apart. Some scientists are studying the possibility that underwater cities may one day be built.

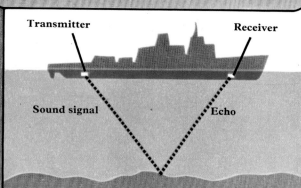

Echo-sounders are used to map the ocean floor. A sound signal is sent from the ship, and its echo is recorded by a receiver. Because the speed of sound through water is known, the depth can be worked out. Ocean mapping has shown that the sea bed is as irregular as the land surface.

Mapping the Ocean Floor

What did the bathyscaph Trieste look like?

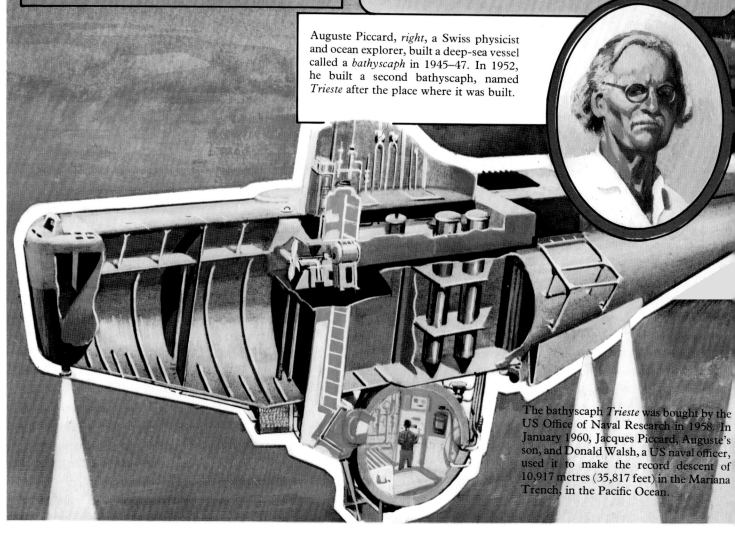

Auguste Piccard, *right*, a Swiss physicist and ocean explorer, built a deep-sea vessel called a *bathyscaph* in 1945–47. In 1952, he built a second bathyscaph, named *Trieste* after the place where it was built.

The bathyscaph *Trieste* was bought by the US Office of Naval Research in 1958. In January 1960, Jacques Piccard, Auguste's son, and Donald Walsh, a US naval officer, used it to make the record descent of 10,917 metres (35,817 feet) in the Mariana Trench, in the Pacific Ocean.

Is underwater exploration possible without machines?

Two Frenchmen, Jacques-Yves Cousteau and Emile Gagnan, developed the aqualung. It enables underwater swimmers to be as mobile as fishes, and to remain underwater for long periods. The cylinders contain compressed air. However, even with an aqualung, swimmers cannot go down much deeper than about 30 metres (100 feet), because of the water pressure.

Can people live on the sea bed?

From the 1960s, scientists have been studying the effects on people of living underwater for some time. The underwater construction called *Tektite I*, *right*, was used in 1969 by four American scientists. They lived in it for two months, some 15 metres (50 feet) below the surface. Such studies will show whether cities may eventually be built on the sea bed.

Is mapping easier today?

Aircraft take photographs in long strips. Detailed maps of the land can be made from these photographs. Each photograph overlaps the next by 60 per cent. The heights of points on the land can be measured by viewing the overlap in 3-D through a stereoscope.

EXPLORATION TODAY After the exploration of Antarctica, there were no new continents to discover. And, accurate mapping of the Earth's surface had been made easier and had been greatly speeded up by the development of air photography. Today, most of the world has been mapped, though some places are mapped in much less detail than others. Air photography became important in World War I, because air photographs showed clearly the position of enemy troops. They are now especially useful in mapping areas of difficult terrain, such as deserts and dense forest regions. However, Man's curiosity remains as great as ever. Some people satisfy their urge to find out about the unknown by exploring caves or mountains. Others attempt feats that no one else has done, such as navigating dangerous rivers or exploring tropical forests. Many explorers today are scientists, such as geologists or biologists. We can share their adventures by seeing the films they make.

What is there to explore beneath the Earth's surface?

The largest caves occur in a rock called limestone, which is dissolved away by rain water. Caves are fascinating and beautiful places. The deepest known cave is in the French Pyrenees mountains, 1,174 metres (3,850 feet) below the surface. Cave exploration can be dangerous. Explorers may be trapped by underground rivers, swollen by sudden heavy rain on the surface.

Have space satellites taught us more about our Earth?

The age of space exploration began in 1957. In that year, the Russians launched *Sputnik I*, an artificial satellite, into orbit around the Earth. Today, satellites send back much information—about the weather, land resources, and so on.

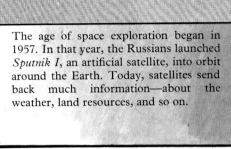

How do modern explorers prepare for an expedition?

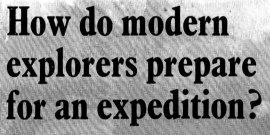

Modern explorers can design their equipment scientifically. *Above*, model boats are tested in a tank in which a strong current of water has been created. The best model is used in designing the boat to be taken on an expedition, *below*. In such ways, scientific research reduces the risk of accidents.

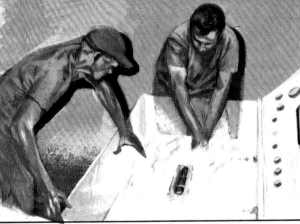

Do mountaineers contribute to exploration?

In the last 100 years or so, mountaineering has become popular. The world's highest mountain, Everest, was conquered in 1953. But there are still many unscaled peaks, especially in the Himalayas. Many more unexplored routes remain to be discovered on other mountains. Special techniques and equipment have made mountaineering less dangerous. But accidents still occur, even among experienced climbers.

A-Z of Exploration

A

Africa North Africa was part of the 'known world' in ancient times. Highlights of modern exploration include:

1488 Bartolomeu Dias rounded the Cape of Good Hope (South Africa).

1497–99 Vasco da Gama sailed around southern Africa to India and back again to Europe.

1618 Pedro Páez discovered the source of the Blue Nile (Ethiopia).

1795–97 and 1805–06 Mungo Park explored the Niger River.

1827–28 René Caillié explored the Sahara.

1841–73 David Livingstone explored south-central Africa.

1858 Richard Burton and John Hanning Speke reached Lake Tanganyika. Speke also saw Lake Victoria.

1874–89 Henry Morton Stanley explored central Africa.

Alexander the Great (356–323 BC), king of Macedon, led a Greek army across south-west Asia to India.

Amundsen, Roald (1872–1928), a Norwegian, discovered the North-West Passage in 1903–06 and became the first person to reach the South Pole (1911).

Antarctica Highlights of exploration:

1831 First undisputed landing by John Biscoe at Cape Ann.

1911 Roald Amundsen reached the South Pole, beating Robert Falcon Scott by a month.

1957–58 Sir Vivian Fuchs led the first Trans-Antarctic Expedition.

Arctic Ocean Highlights of exploration:

1878–79 Nils Nordenskjöld completed a journey through the North-East Passage.

1903–06 Roald Amundsen sailed through the North-West Passage.

1909 Robert E. Peary became the first person to reach the North Pole.

1968–69 Wally Herbert led the first Trans-Arctic Expedition.

astrolabe, an instrument used in navigation to measure the angles of heavenly bodies. It was replaced in modern times by the quadrant and the sextant.

Australia Highlights of exploration:

1606 First recorded discovery of Australia by the Dutchman Willem Jansz.

1642 Abel Tasman discovered Tasmania.

1770 Captain Cook explored the east coast of Australia.

1801–07 Matthew Flinders sailed around Australia.

1860–62 Robert O'Hara Burke and William Wills made the first north–south crossing of the continent.

B

Balboa, Vasco Núñez de (1475–1519), a Spaniard, was the first European to cross Central America (the Isthmus of Panama) and see the Pacific Ocean (1513).

Barth, Heinrich (1821–65), a German, crossed the Sahara and explored west-central Africa for Britain in 1850–55.

Bellingshausen, Fabian von (1778–1852), a Russian sea captain, sailed around Antarctica between 1819 and 1821.

Bering, Vitus (1681–1741), a Dane, explored the Bering Strait and the coasts of Alaska and Siberia in 1727–41.

Brazza, Pierre Savorgnan de (1852–1905), a Frenchman, explored west-central Africa in 1875–83.

Bruce, James (1730–94), a Scotsman, explored Ethiopia and rediscovered the source of the Blue Nile in 1770.

Burke, Robert O'Hara (1821–61), an Irishman, led the first north–south overland journey across Australia in 1860–61. He and one of his companions died on the return journey.

Burton, Sir Richard Francis (1821–90), a British scholar and explorer, travelled in Arabia and north-east Africa. In 1858, with John Hanning Speke, he discovered Lake Tanganyika.

Byrd, Richard Evelyn (1888–1957), an American, explored the Arctic and Antarctic. He flew over the North Pole in 1926 and also became the first man to fly over the South Pole in 1929.

C

Cabot, John (1450–98), an Italian, sailed to Canada for Britain, reaching Newfoundland and Nova Scotia in 1497.

Cabot, Sebastian (1474–1557), son of John Cabot, accompanied his father on the voyage of 1497. In 1509, he reached the entrance to Hudson Bay and later explored South America for Spain.

Caillié René Auguste (1799–1838), a Frenchman, explored the Sahara and parts of western Africa in 1827–28.

caravel was a ship developed by the Spaniards and Portuguese in the 1400s for long sea voyages. Caravels were longer, slimmer, and had larger sails than earlier ships. They were used by Christopher Columbus and many others.

Carthage was a colony established by the Phoenicians in what is now Tunisia, North Africa. The Carthaginians were great explorers and traders. Hanno, a Carthaginian, explored the west coast of Africa in about 500 BC.

Cartier, Jacques (1491–1557), a Frenchman, explored eastern Canada in 1534 and 1535, when he sailed down the St Lawrence River, and again in 1541.

Champlain, Samuel de (1567?–1635), a Frenchman, was an explorer of Canada. He founded the city of Quebec in 1608.

chronometers are extremely accurate clocks, developed in the 1700s. Ships' chronometers usually show Greenwich Mean Time. By comparing GMT with local time, measured by the position of the sun in the sky, navigators work out their longitude, because one hour difference in time represents 15° of longitude.

Clark, William (1770–1838), an American, explored the western United States with Meriwether Lewis in 1804–06. They reached the Pacific coast.

Columbus, Christopher (1451–1506), was born in Genoa (Italy). A skilled seaman, he believed that he could find a short route to Asia by sailing westwards. In August 1492, his expedition, sponsored by Spain, set out. He had three ships, the *Santa Maria, Pinta,* and *Niña.* He sighted the island of San Salvador in the Bahamas on October 12, 1492, but he thought that he had reached Japan. He sailed on to Cuba before returning, in triumph, to Europe. He led three other expeditions: in 1493–96; in 1498–1500, when he sighted South America; and in 1502–04. But, even up to his death, he still thought that he had reached Asia.

compass is an instrument used to measure directions. The first magnetic compasses were invented in China. They probably came into use in Europe in the 1100s.

Cook, James (1728–79), a British sea captain, explored the Pacific Ocean. In 1768–71, he sailed around New Zealand and along eastern Australia. His second voyage (1772–75) took him south of the Antarctic Circle. His last voyage (1776–79) ended when he was killed by the islanders in Hawaii.

Coronado, Francisco Vasquez de (1510–54), a Spaniard, explored what is now the south-western United States in 1540–42. He was searching for cities supposed to be rich in gold.

Cortés, Hernan (1485–1547), a Spaniard landed in Mexico in 1519. By 1521, he had made himself conqueror of the Aztec empire.

Cousteau, Jacques-Yves (1910–), a Frenchman, helped to develop the aqualung, which has made underwater exploration far easier than before. With an aqualung, swimmers are mobile and can remain underwater for long periods.

D

da Gama, Vasco (1469?–1524), a Portuguese mariner, was the first European to find a sea route from Europe, around Africa, to Asia. He set out in 1497, reached

India in 1498 and returned to Portugal in 1499.

De Soto, Hernando (1500?–42), a Spaniard, explored what is now the southeastern United States in 1539–41.

Dias, Bartolomeu (1450–1500), a Portuguese seaman, sailed around southern Africa in 1488. He was drowned when his ship, one of a fleet which discovered Brazil (led by Pedro Cabral), went down in a storm.

Drake, Sir Francis (1540?–96), an English seaman, became the second (after Magellan) to sail around the world (1577–80). He largely followed Magellan's route, and so his contribution to knowledge was not great.

E

Emin Pasha (1840–92) was the name taken by the German Eduard Schnitzer, who was governor of Sudan. He is best known for exploring the upper Nile region.

Eric the Red (950?–1003?), a Norseman, explored Greenland and established a settlement there in 985.

Ericson, Leif (900s–1000s), son of Eric the Red, may have been the first European to land in North America, in 986. However some experts say the first landing was made by another Norseman, Bjarni Herjulfsson. The place which Ericson reached in 1000–01 (Vinland) may have been Cape Cod, in Massachusetts.

F

Flinders, Matthew (1774–1814), an English navigator, sailed around Australia between 1802 and 1803. He proved that Tasmania was an island.

Forrest, Sir John (1847–1918), an Australian, explored west-central Australia between 1869 and 1874.

Franklin, Sir John (1786–1847), a Briton, is known for his Arctic expeditions (in 1819, 1825, and 1845), searching for the North-West Passage. He died with all the members of his expedition, as a result of hardship, when he was close to achieving his aim.

Frobisher, Sir Martin (1535?–94), a Briton, tried three times (in 1576, 1577, and 1578) to find the North-West Passage. He failed, but extended knowledge of north-eastern North America.

Fuchs, Sir Vivian Ernest (1908–), a British geologist, led the first overland Trans-Antarctic Expedition in 1957–58. He travelled 3,450 km (2,140 miles) in 99 days.

G

Greece, ancient The ancient Greeks extended European knowledge of the world and recorded it scientifically. Their knowledge was summarized by Ptolemy in the AD 100s in his book *Geography*.

Hanno (6th–5th cent BC), a Carthaginian, led an expedition to explore the coast of West Africa in about 500 BC. He may have reached the Gulf of Guinea.

Hartog, Dirk (born 1500s), a Dutchman, landed in western Australia in 1616.

Henry the Navigator (1394–1460), the third son of King John I of Portugal, promoted exploration in the 1400s. He did not go on any expeditions himself, but sponsored many. He also encouraged experts to develop navigational aids and to improve ship designs.

Herbert, Walter (Wally) William (1934–), an English explorer, led the first Trans-Arctic Expedition (via the North Pole) in 1968–69. In 1978 he set out to explore the coasts of Greenland.

Hillary, Sir Edmund (1919–), a New Zealander, climbed Mount Everest on May 29, 1953, together with Tensing Norgay, a Sherpa. He also established supply bases in 1957 for the trans-Antarctic crossing by Sir Vivian Fuchs, whom he met at the South Pole.

Hudson, Henry (?–1611), a British sea captain, discovered Hudson Bay and Hudson Strait in 1609–10. He also explored Hudson River in his search for the North-West Passage. On his last voyage, his crew mutinied and he was cast adrift with eight companions in Hudson Bay, never to be heard of again.

Humboldt, Alexander von (1769–1859), a German scientist, explored parts of Central and South America (1799–1804).

J L

Joliet, Louis (1645–1700), a French-Canadian born in Quebec, explored the Mississippi River with Father Jacques Marquette in 1673.

La Salle, Sieur de, Robert Cavelier (1643–87), a Frenchman, became a fur trader in Canada. He explored the Great Lakes region and the Mississippi Valley, which he claimed for France.

latitude and longitude Lines of latitude (or parallels) are drawn on maps parallel to the equator. They are measured from the equator (0° latitude) to the poles (90° North and 90° South). Lines of longitude (or meridians) are at right angles to lines of latitude. They are measured east and west of the prime meridian (0° longitude), which passes through Greenwich in England. The position of any place on Earth is given by stating its latitude and longitude.

Leichhardt, Friedrich Wilhelm Ludwig (1813–48), a Prussian, explored the northern and eastern coastal regions of Australia. He vanished in 1848.

Lewis, Meriwether (1774–1809), an American, explored the western United States in 1804–06 in a series of journeys with William Clark.

Livingstone, Dr David (1813–73), a Scot, explored the interior of south-central Africa, and helped to stop the slave trade there. He went to South Africa in 1840 as a missionary. His achievements as an explorer included the discovery of the Victoria Falls in 1855. He later searched for the source of the River Nile. Henry Morton Stanley went to find him in 1871. He met Livingstone at Ujiji, on Lake Tanganyika, and gave him supplies. Livingstone then went south to Lake Bangweulu (now in Zambia). There, he died.

M

Mackenzie, Alexander (1764–1820), a Scot, explored north-western Canada. He reached the Arctic coast in 1789 and the Pacific Ocean in 1793.

Magellan, Ferdinand (1480–1521), a Portuguese mariner, led the first expedition to sail around the world. He set out in 1519, sailing westwards around South America (via the Strait of Magellan). He finally reached the Philippines, where he was killed. One of his ships, the *Victoria*, reached Seville in 1522. A crew member wrote an account of the voyage.

maps were drawn by explorers to record their travels. The ancient Greeks made maps and developed a system of latitude and longitude. Map-making developed quickly in the 1400s and 1500s. Today, detailed mapping can be done quickly by matching up photographs taken from aircraft.

Marquette, Fr Jacques (1637–75), a French missionary, accompanied Louis Joliet in exploring the Mississippi River. They proved that the river flowed into the Gulf of Mexico.

N

Nansen, Fridtjof (1861–1930), a Norwegian, explored Greenland in 1888 and tried to reach the North Pole in 1893–96 in his ship *Fram*. Locked in the ice, his ship drifted northwards. He left the ship at latitude 84°4′ North and went on foot to latitude 86°14′ North, only 438 km (272 miles) from the North Pole.

Nile River, in Africa, intrigued many explorers in the 1800s, who searched for its source. John Hanning Speke guessed that Lake Victoria was the Nile's source in 1858, but his theory was hotly disputed until other explorers proved that he was correct some years later.

Nordenskjöld, Nils Adolf (1832–1901), a Swede, was the first person to sail through the North-East Passage (1878–79).

North and Central America Highlights of exploration include:

1000–01 Leif Ericson probably landed in North America.

1492 Christopher Columbus landed on San Salvador in the Bahamas.

1497 John Cabot explored east Canada.

1513 Vasco Núñez de Balboa crossed Central America and saw the Pacific from a mountain top.

1521 Hernan Cortés conquered Mexico.

1535 Jacques Cartier sailed up the St Lawrence River.

1539–42 Hernando de Soto explored the south-east and Francisco Vasquez de Coronado the south-west of what is now the United States.

1673 Louis Joliet and Jacques Marquette explored the Mississippi River.

1793 Alexander Mackenzie crossed Canada and reached the Pacific Ocean. He discovered the Mackenzie River.

1804–06 Meriwether Lewis and William Clark crossed the United States and reached the Pacific coast.

North-East Passage was a route sought by explorers from Europe to Asia via the Arctic Ocean. It was finally sailed by Nils Nordenskjöld (1878–79).

North-West Passage was a route sought by explorers around North America to Asia. The journey was successfully accomplished by Roald Amundsen in 1903–06.

O P

Orellana, Francisco de (1500?–49?), a Spaniard, explored the Amazon River in South America in 1541–43, after he had left the expedition of Francisco Pizarro in order to obtain supplies.

Páez, Pedro (1564–1622), a Spaniard, visited Ethiopia in 1603. He saw Lake Tana, the source of the Blue Nile.

Park, Mungo (1771–1806), a Scot, explored the upper Niger River in West Africa in 1795–97 and in 1805–06. He was drowned while trying to escape an African attack. Richard Lander, a Briton, finally proved that the Niger flowed into the Gulf of Guinea in 1830.

Peary, Robert Edwin (1856–1920), an American, became on April 6, 1909, the first person to reach the North Pole. In an earlier expedition, he had proved that Greenland is an island.

Phoenicia lay along the coasts of what are now Israel, Lebanon, and Syria. From about 2700 BC, the Phoenicians were great traders. They explored the Mediterranean and sailed into the Atlantic. The Greek historian Herodotus told of a Phoenician journey around Africa in about 600 BC. But there is no other evidence to support this statement.

Piccard, Auguste (1884–1962), a Swiss inventor, developed the bathyscaph for undersea exploration. His bathyscaph *Trieste*, manned by his son Jacques and Donald Walsh, an American naval officer, reached the record depth of 10,917 metres (35,817 feet) in the Mariana Trench in 1960.

Pizzaro, Francisco (1478?–1541), a Spanish soldier, conquered the Inca empire in Peru in the 1530s.

Pole Star is nearly overhead at the North Pole. In the northern hemisphere, the Pole Star appears to be still, while the other stars appear to circle around it. Sailors use the Pole Star in navigation to find their latitude.

Polo, Marco (1254?–1324?), a Venetian, explored central Asia, China, and southern Asia with his father Nicolò and his uncle Maffeo between 1271 and 1295.

Ptolemy, Claudius, who lived in the AD 100s, was a Greek astronomer and geographer. He summarized the knowledge of the world in his day in a book called *Geography*. Little more was added to European knowledge of the world until the great Age of Exploration began in the 1400s.

Pytheas of Marseille, a Greek navigator, sailed around Britain and then northwards to Scandinavia or, possibly, Iceland in about 325 BC.

R S

Ross, Sir James Clark (1800–62), a Scot, reached the north magnetic pole in 1831. He also explored the Antarctic Ocean between 1839 and 1843.

Scott, Robert Falcon (1868–1912), a Briton, led two Antarctic expeditions. On the second, he reached the South Pole on January 17, 1912, a month after Roald Amundsen. Scott and his companions perished on the return journey only a short distance from safety.

Shackleton, Sir Ernest Henry (1874–1922), an Irishman, got within 156 km (97 miles) of the South Pole in 1908. He led other Antarctic expeditions in 1914–16 and 1921–22.

South America Highlights of exploration:

1498 Christopher Columbus sighted the northern coast of South America.

1499–1500 Amerigo Vespucci explored the eastern coast of South America.

1500 Pedro Alvarez Cabral's fleet discovered what is now Brazil.

1520 Ferdinand Magellan rounded South America and entered the Pacific from the Atlantic.

1530s Francisco Pizzaro seized Peru.

1540–41 Pedro de Valdivia explored and conquered Chile.

1541–43 Francisco de Orellana explored the Amazon River.

Speke, John Hanning (1827–64), a Briton, accompanied Richard Burton on an expedition to find Lake Tanganyika in 1858. Speke went on to Lake Victoria, which he claimed was the source of the Nile. He returned in 1860–62 with James Grant and explored the Lake Victoria region.

Stanley, Sir Henry Morton (1841–1904), was born in Wales but emigrated to the United States. As a newspaper reporter, he sought and found David Livingstone in 1871. Between 1874 and 1889, he led several expeditions in tropical Africa and explored the Congo (now Zaïre) River.

Stuart, John McDouall (1815–66), who was born in Scotland, crossed Australia from south to north in 1862.

Sturt, Charles (1795–1869), an Englishman, explored south-eastern Australia in 1828–30 and the interior in 1844–46.

T V W

Tasman, Abel Janszoon (1603–59), a Dutch navigator, discovered Tasmania and New Zealand in 1642.

Verrazano, Giovanni da (1485?–1528?), an Italian, explored north-eastern North America for France in 1524 in an attempt to find a North-West Passage.

Vespucci, Amerigo (1451–1512), an Italian merchant, explored South America and the West Indies on voyages between 1497 and 1503. The word *America* comes from his first name *Amerigo*.

Wills, William John (1834–61), an Englishman, accompanied Robert O'Hara Burke on the overland expedition across Australia in 1860–61. He died of malnutrition on the return journey.

RACE FOR THE Moon

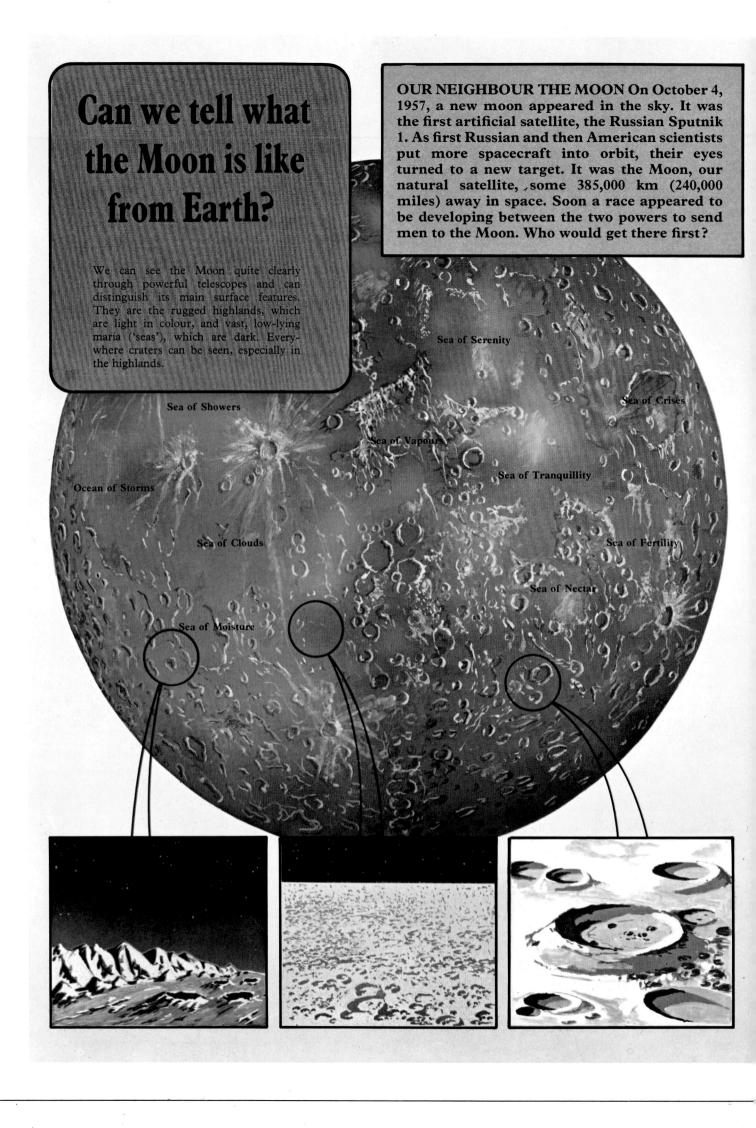

Can we tell what the Moon is like from Earth?

We can see the Moon quite clearly through powerful telescopes and can distinguish its main surface features. They are the rugged highlands, which are light in colour, and vast, low-lying maria ('seas'), which are dark. Everywhere craters can be seen, especially in the highlands.

OUR NEIGHBOUR THE MOON On October 4, 1957, a new moon appeared in the sky. It was the first artificial satellite, the Russian Sputnik 1. As first Russian and then American scientists put more spacecraft into orbit, their eyes turned to a new target. It was the Moon, our natural satellite, some 385,000 km (240,000 miles) away in space. Soon a race appeared to be developing between the two powers to send men to the Moon. Who would get there first?

Sea of Serenity

Sea of Crises

Sea of Showers

Sea of Vapours

Sea of Tranquillity

Ocean of Storms

Sea of Clouds

Sea of Fertility

Sea of Nectar

Sea of Moisture

How do spacecraft help in studying the Moon?

Spacecraft can approach much closer to the Moon, and even land on it. They can photograph its surface in minute detail and spot things we cannot see from Earth. They can return to Earth with samples of Moon soil. They can view the far side of the Moon, which we can never see from Earth.

Do we know where the Moon came from?

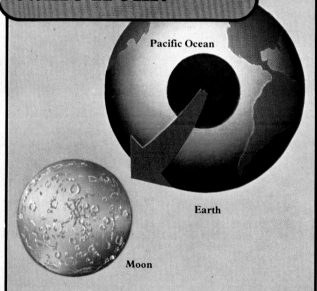

Pacific Ocean

Earth

Moon

There are several different ideas about how the Moon came into being. For a long time people thought that it was torn from the Earth, from the region that is now the Pacific Ocean. But scientists think this is most unlikely. They think that the Moon probably formed as a separate body at the same time as the Earth.

Why should man go to the Moon?

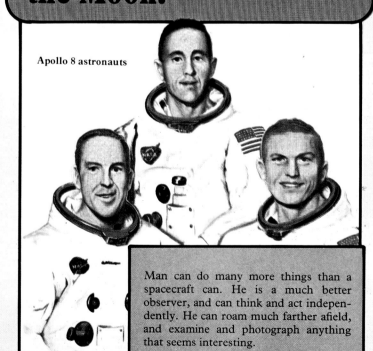

Apollo 8 astronauts

Man can do many more things than a spacecraft can. He is a much better observer, and can think and act independently. He can roam much farther afield, and examine and photograph anything that seems interesting.

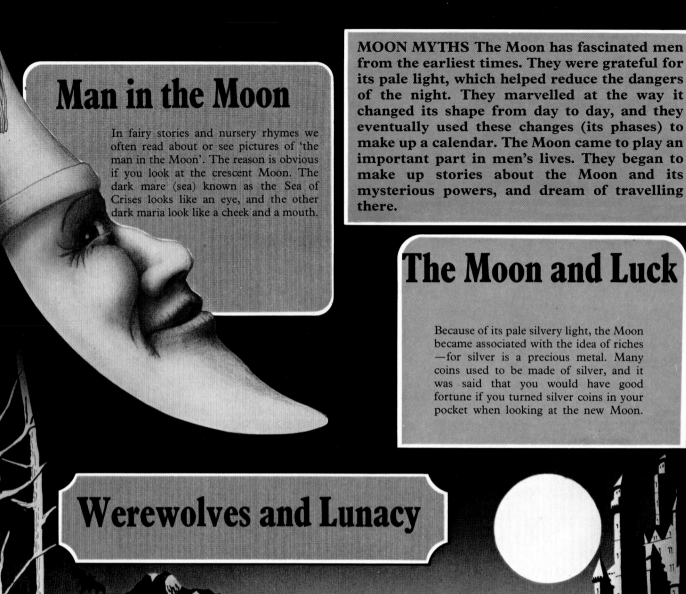

Man in the Moon

In fairy stories and nursery rhymes we often read about or see pictures of 'the man in the Moon'. The reason is obvious if you look at the crescent Moon. The dark mare (sea) known as the Sea of Crises looks like an eye, and the other dark maria look like a cheek and a mouth.

MOON MYTHS The Moon has fascinated men from the earliest times. They were grateful for its pale light, which helped reduce the dangers of the night. They marvelled at the way it changed its shape from day to day, and they eventually used these changes (its phases) to make up a calendar. The Moon came to play an important part in men's lives. They began to make up stories about the Moon and its mysterious powers, and dream of travelling there.

The Moon and Luck

Because of its pale silvery light, the Moon became associated with the idea of riches —for silver is a precious metal. Many coins used to be made of silver, and it was said that you would have good fortune if you turned silver coins in your pocket when looking at the new Moon.

Werewolves and Lunacy

A more widely held belief was that the light from the full Moon could affect the mind. Madness could result. Another word for madness—lunacy—comes from the Latin word for Moon. From eastern Europe came tales of how men changed into wolves ('werewolves') at the time of the full Moon. There is no truth in either of these ideas.

Diana the Moon Goddess

Most of the early civilizations worshipped the Moon, which was thought to possess strange powers. The Romans called their Moon goddess Diana. She was one of the most important deities and was also goddess of the hunt. The crescent Moon was her bow, and moonbeams were her arrows.

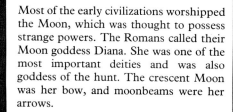

The Moon and Weather

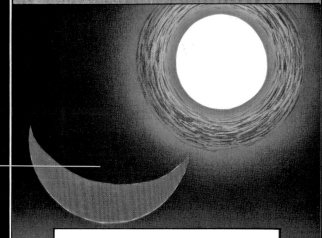

Many country folk believe that you can foretell the weather from the appearance of the Moon. A halo around the Moon and 'the Moon on its back' are signs of bad weather. They also say that the phases of the Moon affect the weather.

In Literature

French writer Cyrano de Bergerac (1619–1655), famed for the length of his nose, was one of the earliest science fiction writers. In one story he tells how he was propelled to the Moon by firecrackers.

The French novelist Jules Verne (1828–1905) wrote stirring tales of trips to the Moon in *From the Earth to the Moon* and *Round the Moon*. Their heroes were launched to the Moon by cannon.

A little later in England, H. G. Wells (1866–1946) 'sent' two men to the Moon in his book *First Men in the Moon*. They went in a spacecraft which they propelled by manipulating the force of gravity.

Is it difficult to escape from Earth's pull?

REACHING FOR THE MOON (1) Sending spacecraft to the Moon requires a lot more power than putting a satellite into orbit. In orbit, a satellite is still firmly held in the grip of the Earth's gravity. It simply balances this gravity by virtue of its speed. To reach the Moon, a spacecraft has to escape from the Earth's gravity and let itself be drawn instead by the gravity of the Moon.

A spacecraft can escape from the powerful grip of gravity only if it is launched towards the skies at a very fast speed—about 40,000 kph (25,000 mph). This speed is known as the *escape velocity*.

Escape velocity 40,000 kph

Orbital velocity 28,000 kph

How do you aim at the Moon?

You cannot send a spacecraft to the Moon by aiming it straight at the Moon. For one thing, a spacecraft always travels in a curve. And the Moon is a moving target. As a result, you must aim the spacecraft so that it arrives at a point in space at the same time as the Moon.

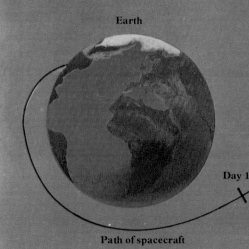

Earth

Day 2

Day 1

Path of spacecraft

Day 2

Day 1

Moon travelling in orbit

Race for the Moon 3

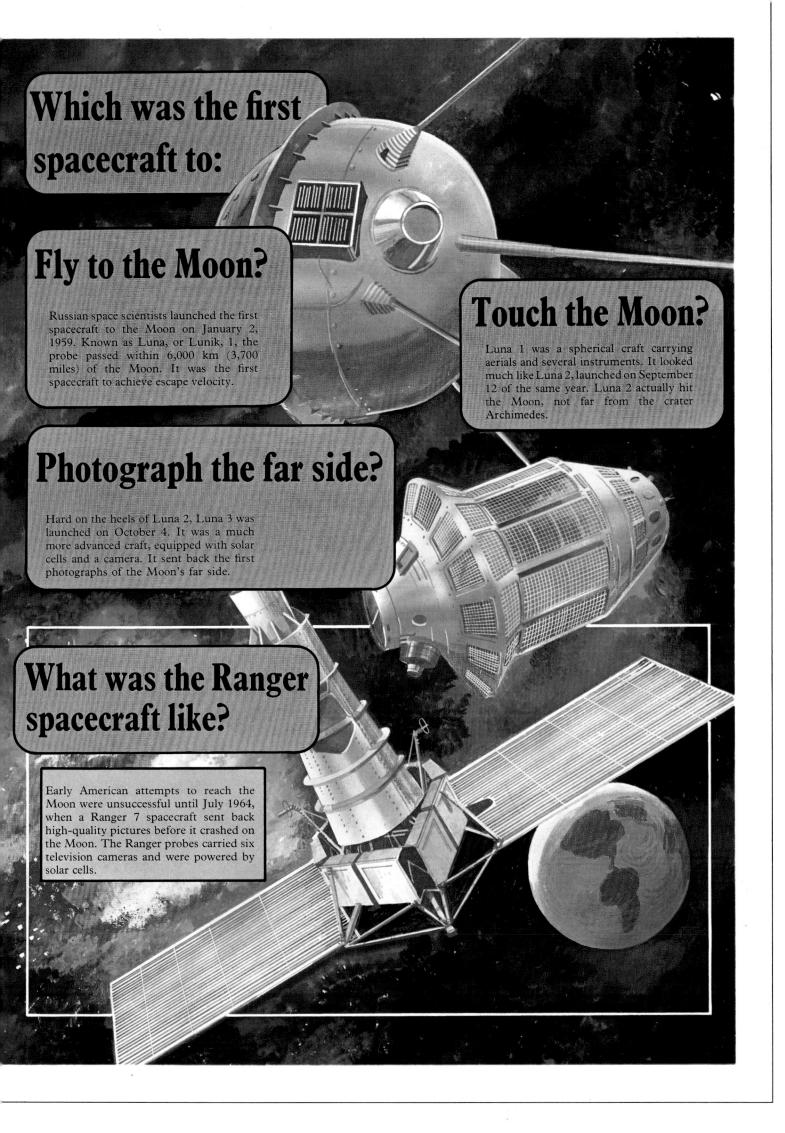

Which was the first spacecraft to:

Fly to the Moon?

Russian space scientists launched the first spacecraft to the Moon on January 2, 1959. Known as Luna, or Lunik, 1, the probe passed within 6,000 km (3,700 miles) of the Moon. It was the first spacecraft to achieve escape velocity.

Touch the Moon?

Luna 1 was a spherical craft carrying aerials and several instruments. It looked much like Luna 2, launched on September 12 of the same year. Luna 2 actually hit the Moon, not far from the crater Archimedes.

Photograph the far side?

Hard on the heels of Luna 2, Luna 3 was launched on October 4. It was a much more advanced craft, equipped with solar cells and a camera. It sent back the first photographs of the Moon's far side.

What was the Ranger spacecraft like?

Early American attempts to reach the Moon were unsuccessful until July 1964, when a Ranger 7 spacecraft sent back high-quality pictures before it crashed on the Moon. The Ranger probes carried six television cameras and were powered by solar cells.

How can we soft-land a spacecraft on the Moon?

After the Luna and Ranger successes in hitting the Moon, space scientists began designing probes that would land gently on the Moon. Soft-landing probes must have a rocket motor to slow them down before they reach the surface.

Which spacecraft first soft-landed on the Moon?

The Russians were the first to soft-land a spacecraft on the Moon, in February 1966. It was in the form of an instrument capsule released by the main spacecraft, Luna 9. It sent back the first close-up pictures of the lunar landscape.

Can parachutes be used to slow a spacecraft down?

When spacecraft return to the Earth after a space flight, they use parachutes to help slow them down. This is possible because the Earth has air around it. The Moon has no air, so parachutes cannot be used. Firing retro-rockets towards the surface is the only way to brake probes for a soft-landing.

What did Surveyor tell us?

It could be argued that the Luna 9 landing was not a true soft-landing. But those of the later American Surveyor probes certainly were. From the way they landed, scientists knew that the lunar surface must be firm. The surface material seemed to be like fine soil on Earth.

Why were the Lunar Orbiters so important?

With each new lunar probe, scientists began to get a much clearer picture of what the Moon was like. Their next step was to put probes into lunar orbit. Most successful were the US Lunar Orbiters, which mapped the whole surface in great detail, especially the proposed sites for the Apollo landings.

What was the Mercury spacecraft like?

BEFORE APOLLO In 1961 the Russians put the first man into orbit—Yuri Gagarin on April 12. Within a month the American president, John F. Kennedy, firmly committed the American people to a manned Moon landing 'by 1970'. Their first man in orbit was John H. Glenn, on February 20, 1962, flying in a Mercury spacecraft. Other Mercury and later Gemini flights paved the way for the ambitious Apollo Moon-landing project.

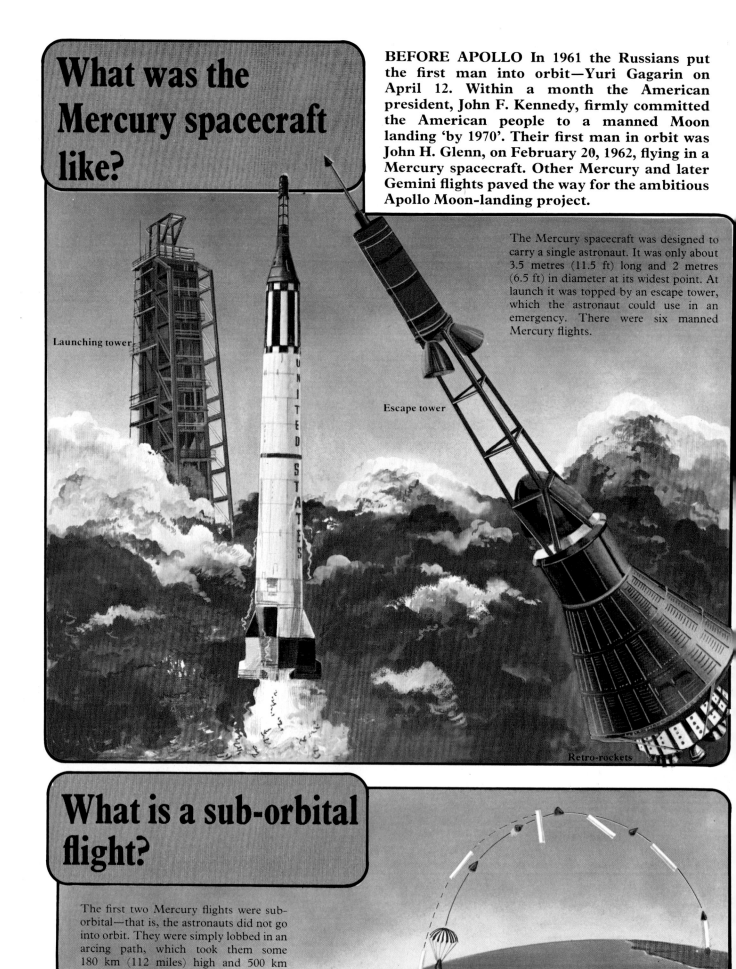

The Mercury spacecraft was designed to carry a single astronaut. It was only about 3.5 metres (11.5 ft) long and 2 metres (6.5 ft) in diameter at its widest point. At launch it was topped by an escape tower, which the astronaut could use in an emergency. There were six manned Mercury flights.

Launching tower

Escape tower

Retro-rockets

What is a sub-orbital flight?

The first two Mercury flights were sub-orbital—that is, the astronauts did not go into orbit. They were simply lobbed in an arcing path, which took them some 180 km (112 miles) high and 500 km (310 miles) from the launching site.

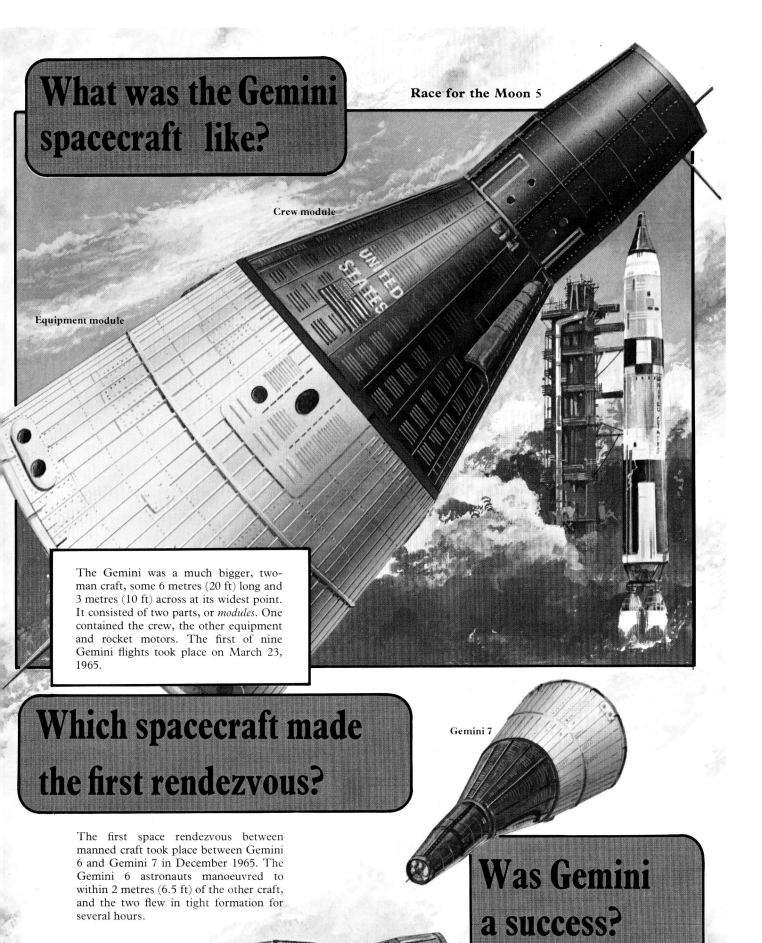

What was the Gemini spacecraft like?

Crew module

Equipment module

The Gemini was a much bigger, two-man craft, some 6 metres (20 ft) long and 3 metres (10 ft) across at its widest point. It consisted of two parts, or *modules*. One contained the crew, the other equipment and rocket motors. The first of nine Gemini flights took place on March 23, 1965.

Which spacecraft made the first rendezvous?

Gemini 7

The first space rendezvous between manned craft took place between Gemini 6 and Gemini 7 in December 1965. The Gemini 6 astronauts manoeuvred to within 2 metres (6.5 ft) of the other craft, and the two flew in tight formation for several hours.

Was Gemini a success?

Gemini was a spectacular success on all counts. By the end of the programme, the United States had overtaken Russia in the number of man-hours spent in space.

Gemini 6

How was Apollo able to reach the Moon and return?

PROJECT APOLLO (1) By the end of 1966 the Gemini astronauts had shown that it was possible to rendezvous and dock (link up) with other spacecraft and 'walk' in space. In 1967 three astronauts were killed during training inside an Apollo spacecraft, and this caused delay while the craft was redesigned. The first manned Apollo flight took place in October 1968, and two months later Apollo 8 made a triumphant circumnavigation of the Moon. The stage was set for the first Moon landing.

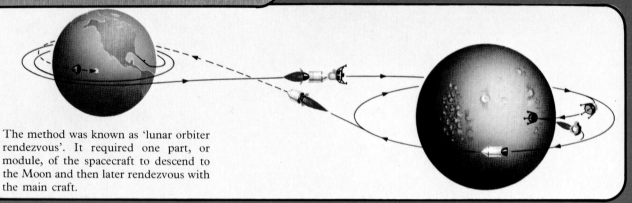

The method was known as 'lunar orbiter rendezvous'. It required one part, or module, of the spacecraft to descend to the Moon and then later rendezvous with the main craft.

What was the Command Module?

The Apollo spacecraft was made up of three modules in all. The three astronauts forming the crew were housed in quite cramped conditions in what was called the Command Module. The module was pressurized and had a thick heat shield to protect the astronauts.

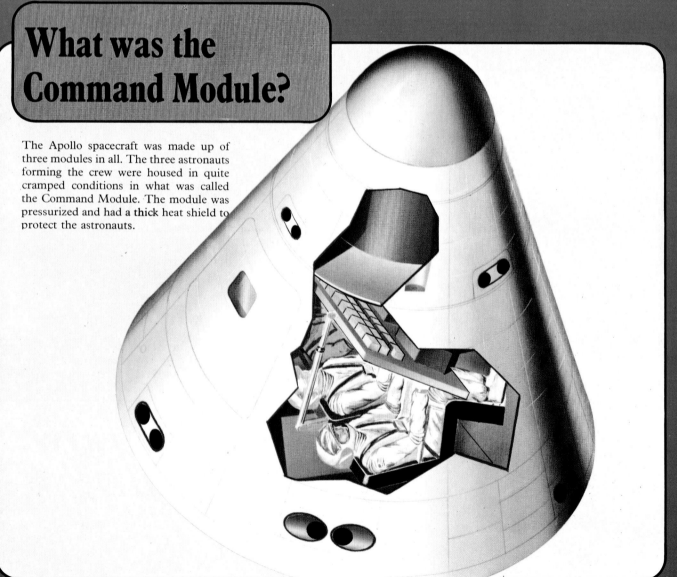

What was the Service Module?

The Service Module was attached to the base of the Command Module. It housed a powerful rocket motor and propellant tanks, together with fuel cells to make electricity, and other equipment.

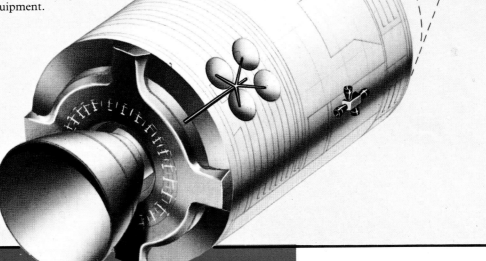

What was the Lunar Module?

The Lunar Module was the part that descended to the Moon's surface with two astronauts inside. In the flight to the Moon it was attached to the Command Module, as shown in the picture on the right.

How big were the modules?

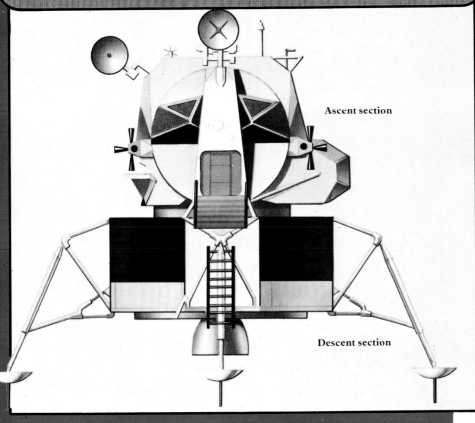

Ascent section

Descent section

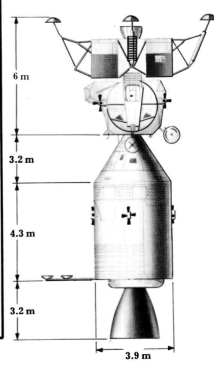

6 m

3.2 m

4.3 m

3.2 m

3.9 m

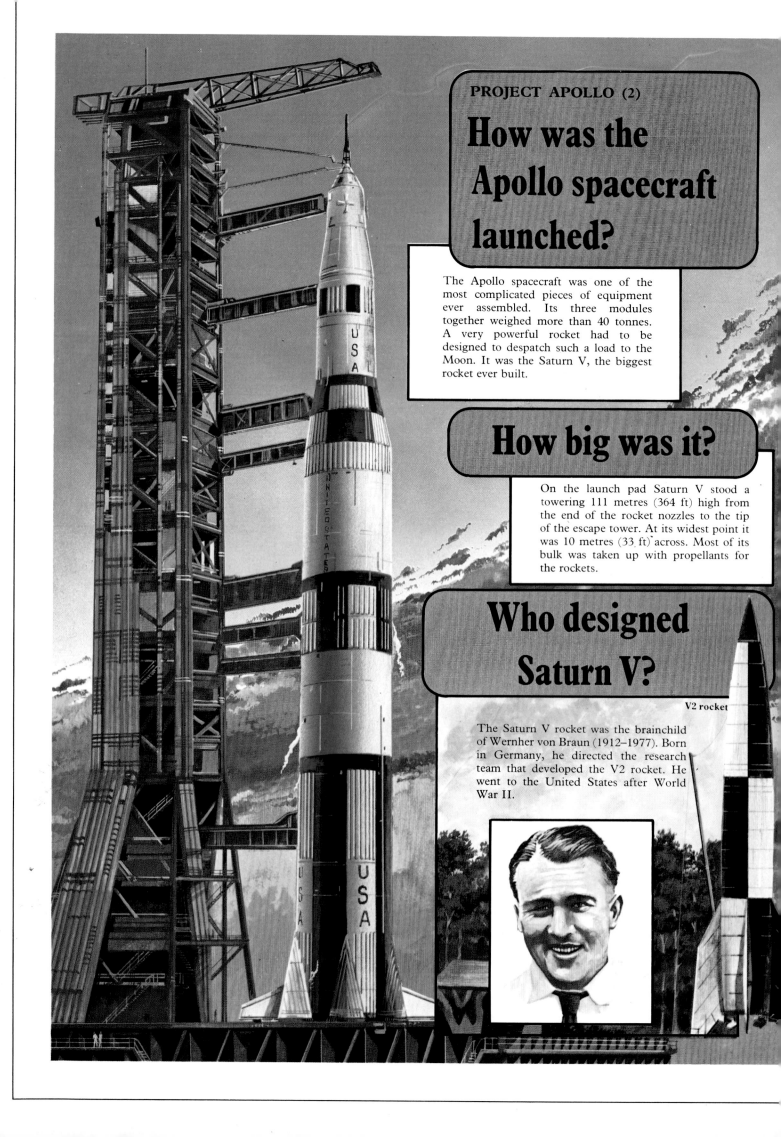

How was the Apollo spacecraft launched?

The Apollo spacecraft was one of the most complicated pieces of equipment ever assembled. Its three modules together weighed more than 40 tonnes. A very powerful rocket had to be designed to despatch such a load to the Moon. It was the Saturn V, the biggest rocket ever built.

How big was it?

On the launch pad Saturn V stood a towering 111 metres (364 ft) high from the end of the rocket nozzles to the tip of the escape tower. At its widest point it was 10 metres (33 ft) across. Most of its bulk was taken up with propellants for the rockets.

Who designed Saturn V?

V2 rocket

The Saturn V rocket was the brainchild of Wernher von Braun (1912–1977). Born in Germany, he directed the research team that developed the V2 rocket. He went to the United States after World War II.

How many stages did Saturn have?

3rd stage

2nd stage motors

1st stage motors

Apollo spacecraft

3rd stage motor

2nd stage

1st stage

Saturn V was a three-stage rocket, which had a total take-off weight of some 2,700 tonnes. Its first-stage rockets burned kerosene and liquid oxygen. The rockets of the other stages used liquid hydrogen as fuel.

Where was it assembled?

Assembly of Saturn V took place in the Vehicle Assembly Building at the Kennedy Space Center in Florida, 5 km (3 miles) from the launch pad. One of the biggest buildings in the world, it has a length of 218 metres (715 ft), a width of 158 metres (518 ft), and a height of 160 metres (525 ft).

How was it moved to the launch pad?

Inside the Vehicle Assembly Building the Saturn rocket was assembled, with launch pad and tower, on top of the biggest vehicle in the world. This was a massive crawler transporter, whose top speed was 0.6 kph (0.4 mph).

DESTINATION MOON (1) The preparations for the Apollo flights to the Moon were lengthy and painstaking. Nothing could be left to chance. The multitude of systems in the spacecraft and its launching rocket were checked and rechecked as the countdown began a few days before launching. Finally all was ready. The rocket motors were ignited, and the huge rocket climbed into the sky.

How long did it take Apollo to get into orbit?

From the moment of ignition of the first-stage engines, it took Saturn V only 12 minutes to boost Apollo into orbit. By this time it had dropped its first two stages and its third stage had shut off. Apollo was then travelling at 28,000 kph (17,000 mph).

Third stage shuts off
Spacecraft is in orbit
12 minutes after lift-off

Why did it go into a parking orbit?

Second stage separates
Third stage fires
9 minutes after lift-off

Escape tower separates

First stage separates
Second stage fires
2½ minutes after lift-off

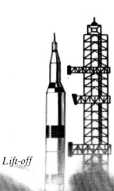

Lift-off

Apollo was put into a so-called parking orbit—rather than sent directly to the Moon—for safety's sake. While in orbit, the astronauts checked out all spacecraft systems to make sure they worked perfectly. Only then did they head for the Moon.

NAME	SURNAME	ADDRESS	DOB	AGE	SEX	PHONE NO	TITLE
KELLY	THOMPSON	3 LICHFIELD ROAD	06/07/76	17	F	081-569-3456	MRS
ANITA	JOMMA	35 ERTA GARDENS,LONDON	03/03/90	3	F	081-430-3467	MISS
GREGORY	CHESTER	43 VICTORIA AVENUE	25/05/77	16	M	081-902-8799	MR
SUE	THOMPSON	43, KILBURN PARK ROAD	10/21/76	17	F	071-625-4433	MISS
SAAD	MIAH	34 ERDON AVENUE	31/09/76	16	M	081-452-9902	MR
RUZWAN	AKRAM	3 ANSON ROAD	31/09/75	18	M	081-452-6657	MR
CHRISTOPHER	TOLKIN	54, KILBURN HIGH ROAD	02/02/78	28	M	071-625-9986	MR
ANGELA	BLAMSBURY	31, MANOR PARK DRIVE	21/11/65	28	F	071-208-1202	DR

What manoeuvres did the astronauts have to make?

After firing the third-stage motor to boost them towards the Moon, the astronauts had to manoeuvre their craft into the correct flight position. The Apollo Command Module had to do an about-turn and link with the Lunar Module, before pulling it clear of the unwanted third stage.

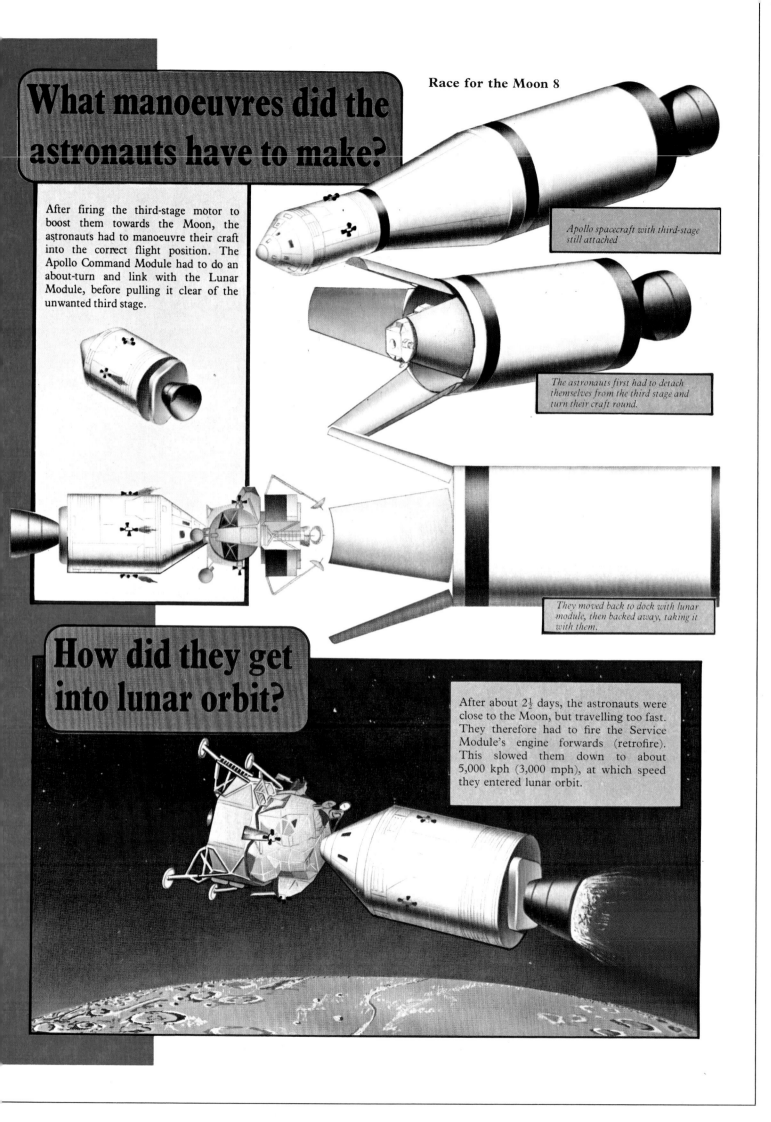

Apollo spacecraft with third-stage still attached

The astronauts first had to detach themselves from the third stage and turn their craft round.

They moved back to dock with lunar module, then backed away, taking it with them.

How did they get into lunar orbit?

After about 2½ days, the astronauts were close to the Moon, but travelling too fast. They therefore had to fire the Service Module's engine forwards (retrofire). This slowed them down to about 5,000 kph (3,000 mph), at which speed they entered lunar orbit.

How did the astronauts descend to the Moon?

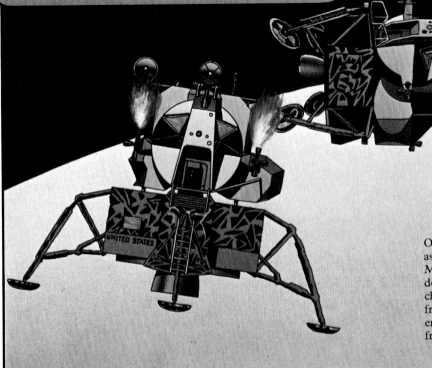

Once in lunar orbit two of the three astronauts climbed into the Lunar Module (LM), in which they would descend to the Moon's surface. Having checked all its systems, they separated from the main craft. They fired the LM's engine to slow it down so that it dropped from orbit, and headed for the surface.

How did they land?

The astronauts also had to fire the LM's engine as a brake so that it could land softly on the surface. There was no other way of slowing it down. Parachutes could not be used, of course, because there is no air on the Moon.

Did they 'fly' the Lunar Module?

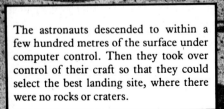

The astronauts descended to within a few hundred metres of the surface under computer control. Then they took over control of their craft so that they could select the best landing site, where there were no rocks or craters.

What did the Lunar Module look like on the Moon?

The Lunar Module was a curious-looking contraption, but it worked well. The sprung, spidery legs cushioned the landing, and the foot pads stopped them from sinking too far into the lunar soil. Much of the body was covered with shiny gold foil to protect it from the Sun's heat.

Where did the landings take place?

Six lunar landings took place in the Apollo Project. The sites are marked on this map:
Apollo 11—Sea of Tranquillity
Apollo 12—Ocean of Storms
Apollo 14—Fra Mauro crater
Apollo 15—Sea of Rains
Apollo 16—Cayley Plains
Apollo 17—Sea of Serenity

Who first walked on the Moon?

Astronaut Neil Armstrong was the first man to set foot on the Moon, on July 21, 1969. He was born at Wapakoneta, in the State of Ohio, in 1930, and became an aeronautical engineer and later a test pilot.

What did he say?

As Neil Armstrong stepped down onto the Moon's dusty surface, hundreds of millions of TV viewers back on Earth waited for his first words: 'That's one small step for a man, one giant leap for mankind.'

Was it difficult to walk on the Moon?

Because of the Moon's low gravity (about one-sixth of the Earth's), the astronauts at first found it difficult to move around. They soon found that it was best to move in a kind of loping gait, rather like a kangaroo.

THE MOON-WALKERS In July 1969 American astronauts achieved the goal President Kennedy had set them in 1961—they set foot on the Moon. Between then and December 1972 six pairs of astronauts—perhaps we should call them 'lunarnauts'—roamed the lunar surface for a total of 166 hours and covered nearly 100 km (about 60 miles). A new era had begun in the history of mankind.

Who was his partner?

Second man on the Moon was Edwin 'Buzz' Aldrin, who was born at Montclair, New Jersey, also in 1930. On the Moon he was snapped in this famous photograph by Armstrong, who is seen reflected in his visor.

What did the Earth look like from the Moon?

The Apollo astronauts took thousands of stunning colour photographs of the Moon. Some showed their home planet, the Earth. The Earth looked beautiful—swirls of white cloud could clearly be seen against the blue of the sea and sky, and the brown of the continents.

Did the men on the Moon have any transport?

Footprints on the Moon

The first two teams of astronauts explored the Moon on foot. The Apollo 14 astronauts used a trolley to carry equipment. The last three teams had the use of a 'lunar buggy', which allowed them to roam several kilometres away from their lander.

The footprints left behind in the soft lunar soil by the 12 astronauts who landed will be preserved for centuries in the weatherless environment.

What kinds of things did the astronauts do on the Moon?

LUNARNAUTS AT WORK The Apollo astronauts had a heavy workload to get through during their relatively brief stay on the Moon. But for months beforehand they had been practising the techniques they had to use. Considering how cumbersome their spacesuits were, they performed their tasks most efficiently, with few mishaps. And they proved to be excellent photographers.

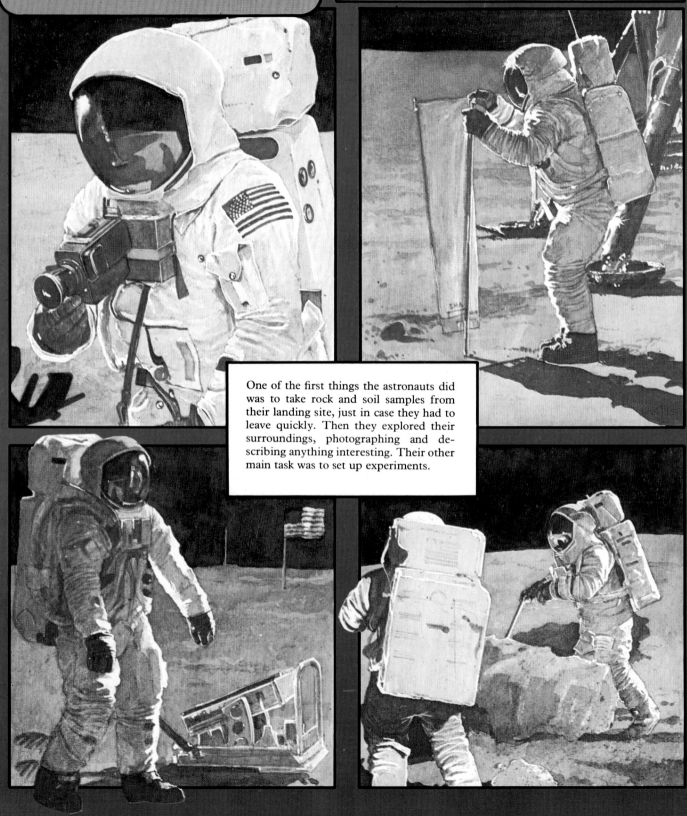

One of the first things the astronauts did was to take rock and soil samples from their landing site, just in case they had to leave quickly. Then they explored their surroundings, photographing and describing anything interesting. Their other main task was to set up experiments.

What experiments did they set up?

They set up experiments to measure such things as waves through the lunar crust ('moonquakes'), the heat the Moon gives out, the presence of atomic particles, and magnetism. The instruments they left behind carried on sending information for years afterwards.

What did they bring back?

The Apollo astronauts brought back a total of no less than 385 kg (850 lb) of Moon rock and soil samples from the six different landing sites. The rock, from both highland and mare (sea) regions, has still not all been investigated thoroughly.

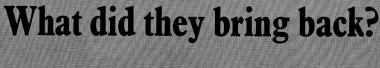

Race for the Moon 11

HOMEWARD BOUND The journey home from the Moon was just as hazardous as the journey out. The two moonwalkers had to return to the main spacecraft, which had to follow a precise flight path back. To hit the Earth's atmosphere at the wrong angle would have caused them to bounce off it or burn up in it. Either would have meant certain death.

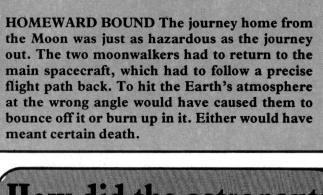

How did the astronauts get off the Moon?

After their exciting and exhausting explorations of the Moon, the astronauts had to rejoin their colleague, who had been circling above them in the main part of the Apollo spacecraft. They blasted off from the Moon in the upper part of the lander, using the lower half as a launch pad.

How did they return to Earth?

The moment of launch was timed so that the lander would meet the main craft circling above. Then the astronauts manoeuvred into position so that they could dock (link up) with the main craft. They then transferred to it, and sent the empty lander back to crash on the Moon. After final checks on the main craft's systems, the astronauts fired its rocket motor to boost it away from the Moon and into a flight path that would take it back to Earth.

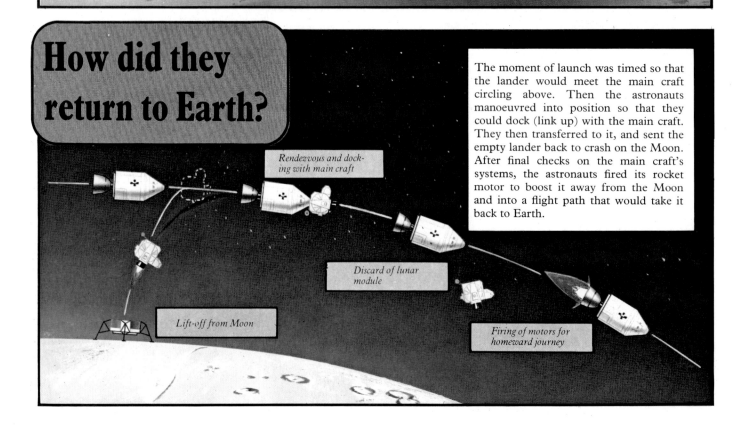

Rendezvous and dock-
ing with main craft

Discard of lunar
module

Lift-off from Moon

Firing of motors for
homeward journey

Unlucky Thirteenth

The third Moon mission—Apollo 13—was indeed unlucky, and the astronauts were fortunate to return alive. Some 300,000 km (200,000 miles) from Earth an explosion occurred in the Service Module. They had to use the power and oxygen of the lander to survive.

How fast did they re-enter the Earth's atmosphere?

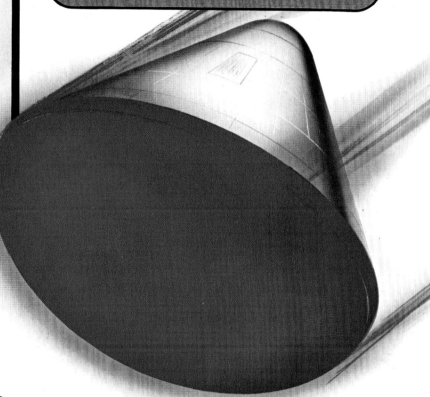

By the time the Apollo astronauts reached the Earth on their return journey, they were travelling at a speed of nearly 40,000 kph (25,000 mph)—or 11 km (7 miles) every second! They separated their Command Module from the Service Module, and plunged into the outer atmosphere—heat shield blazing.

How did they land?

The atmosphere acted like a brake and quickly slowed the Command Module down. Then parachutes opened above the craft to slow it down further. All of the Apollo landings were at sea, and recovery vessels were close at hand to remove the astronauts as quickly as possible.

What are Moon rocks like?

Microscopic cross-section of Moon rock

The Moon rocks can broadly be divided into two types. One is dark and quite similar to basalt on Earth. The other consists of a mixture of rock chips cemented together, rather like breccia on Earth.

AFTER APOLLO The whole Apollo project is estimated to have cost more than $US25,000 million. But the scientific benefits from the Moon trips have been enormous. And the project accelerated the growth of new technologies, such as micro-electronics, which led to the introduction of pocket calculators. Many of the Moon's mysteries, however, remain, so men will continue to investigate this barren, lifeless world.

What have they told us?

The Moon rocks are quite different in composition from Earth rocks. This indicates that the Moon almost certainly did not come from the Earth. The mare (sea) samples are much younger than those from the highlands, which are thought to be part of the Moon's original crust. The maria were probably formed when huge meteorites crashed into the crust and caused it to remelt.

Race for the Moon 13

What was the Luna spacecraft like?

The USSR did not send any manned spacecraft to the Moon. Instead, they built and launched the Luna spacecraft, a robot craft designed to soft-land on the lunar surface. It was equipped with a moveable arm fitted with a drill which bored into the Moon's surface.

What is special about them?

The drill bores into the surface and extracts a sample of soil. The arm delivers this into a capsule on top of the spacecraft. The upper part of the craft then takes off and returns the capsule to Earth.

What else has been landed on the Moon?

The most ingenious device the Russians have sent to the Moon is the robot vehicle called Lunokhod. The first one landed on the Moon in November 1970. Lunokhod is driven by electric motors. The electricity comes from solar cells in its 'lid'. It is guided by scientists back on Earth, who 'see' through its twin television cameras.

MOON BASE It is only a question of time before man returns to the Moon to set up a permanent base. Because of its airless skies, the Moon would make an ideal site for a deep space observatory, for example. Its first inhabitants will be scientists and engineers, but it will soon expand into a flourishing colony.

How will the first Moon base be built?

The first Moon base will be a simple construction. Probably it will be put together from the empty casings of the rockets used to propel the construction engineers to the Moon. The casings will be fitted out with extra equipment for their new role.

How will permanent bases be constructed?

A permanent Moon base will be built mainly underground, using tunnelling machines 'imported' from Earth. Beneath the ground, the Moon colonists will be protected from the scorching heat of the lunar day and the deathly cold of the lunar night.

Will they be self-supporting?

For a while, the Moon base will depend on Earth for all of its materials—oxygen, water, food, and equipment. But soon the colonists will begin to help support themselves. They will start growing their own food in vast greenhouses. They will recycle their water and wastes. They will begin mining their own raw materials for building and making metals. And they will set up chains of solar power stations to give them electricity.

Why will a Moon base be a good space port?

When journeys to other planets and space cities become common, the Moon will act as a major space port—for refuelling operations and transfer of passengers and cargo. Because of its low gravity, spaceships would be able to come and go more easily than they could on Earth.

US Manned Spaceflights (to the end of Project Apollo)

Mission	Date	Crew	Duration (hours)	Remarks
Mercury 3	May 5, 1961	Shepard	0.25	Suborbital flight–first American in space. (Spacecraft call sign Freedom 7)
Mercury 4	July 21, 1961	Grissom	0.25	Also suborbital; successful flight but spacecraft sank, astronaut rescued. (Liberty Bell 7)
Mercury 6	Feb. 20, 1962	Glenn	4.9	Three-orbit flight; first American in orbit; retropack retained when erroneous signal indicated heat shield possibly loose; capsule landed 60 km (37 miles) uprange. (Friendship 7)
Mercury 7	May 24, 1962	Carpenter	4.9	Also three-orbit mission; yaw error at manual retrofire caused 400-km (250-mile) landing overshoot. (Aurora 7)
Mercury 8	Oct. 3, 1962	Schirra	9.2	Six-orbit flight; capsule landed 6 km (4 miles) from recovery ship. (Sigma 7)
Mercury 9	May 15–16, 1963	Cooper	34.3	Twenty-two orbits to evaluate effects on man of one day in space. (Faith 7)
Gemini 3	March 23, 1965	Grissom, Young	4.9	Three-orbit demonstration of the new spacecraft; manoeuvre over Texas on first pass changed orbital path of a manned spacecraft for first time; landed about 80 km (50 miles) uprange. (Molly Brown, only Gemini named)
Gemini 4	June 3–7, 1965	McDivitt, White	97.9	Four-day flight with White first American to walk in space, in 20-minute extravehicular activity (EVA); after 62 revolutions of Earth, landed 80 km (50 miles) uprange.
Gemini 5	Aug. 21–29, 1965	Cooper, Conrad	190.9	First use of fuel cells for electric power; evaluated guidance and navigation system for future rendezvous missions; incorrect navigation co-ordinates from ground control resulted in landing 140 km (87 miles) short; 120 revolutions.
Gemini 7	Dec. 4–18, 1965	Borman, Lovell	330.6	Longest Gemini flight; provided rendezvous target for Gemini 6; crew flew portions of mission in shirtsleeves for first time; 206 revolutions.
Gemini 6	Dec. 15–16, 1965	Schirra, Stafford	25.8	Rescheduled to rendezvous with Gemini 7 after original target Agena unmanned spacecraft failed to orbit; 6 launch postponed 3 days when launch vehicle engines automatically shut down 1.2 seconds after ignition; completed first space rendezvous; 16 revolutions.
Gemini 8	March 16, 1966	Armstrong, Scott	10.7	First docking of one space vehicle with another; about 27 minutes after docking, Gemini-Agena combination began to yaw and roll at increasing rates; mission was terminated midway through 7th revolution.
Gemini 9	June 3–6, 1966	Stafford, Cernan	72.4	Rescheduled to rendezvous and dock with augmented target docking adapter after original target Agena failed to orbit; docking proved impossible but three different types of rendezvous were completed; Cernan carried out more than 2 hours EVA: 44 revolutions.

Mission	Crew	Date	Duration (hours)	Remarks
Gemini 10	Young, Collins	July 18–21, 1966	70.8	First use of Agena target vehicle's propulsion systems; spacecraft also rendezvoused with Gemini 8 target vehicle; Collins had 49 minutes EVA standing in hatch, 39-minute EVA to retrieve experiment from Agena 8; 43 revolutions.
Gemini 11	Conrad, Gordon	Sept. 12–15, 1966	71.3	Gemini record altitude (1,190 km; 739 miles) reached using Agena propulsion system after first-revolution rendezvous and docking, Gordon fastened Agena-anchored tether to Gemini docking bar, and spacecraft later made two revolutions of Earth in tethered configuration; Gordon 33-minute EVA and 2-hour plus standup EVA; 44 revolutions.
Gemini 12	Lovell, Aldrin	Nov. 11–15, 1966	94.6	Final Gemini flight; Aldrin logged Gemini record total of $5\frac{1}{2}$ hours extravehicular activity; 59 revolutions.
Apollo 7	Schirra, Eisele, Cunningham	Oct. 11–22, 1968	260.2	First manned flight of Apollo spacecraft Command and Service Module only; 163 revolutions. Like the subsequent Apollo spacecraft, it splashed down within 15 km (9 miles) of predicted landing point.
Apollo 8	Borman, Lovell, Anders	Dec. 21–27, 1968	147.0	First flight to the Moon (CSM only); views of lunar surface televised to Earth; 10 revolutions of the Moon.
Apollo 9	McDivitt, Scott, Schweickart	March 3–13, 1969	241.0	First manned flight of Lunar Module (LM); spacecraft call signs for communications identification when undocked: CSM 'Gumdrop' and LM 'Spider'; Schweickart 37-minute EVA from LM; 151 revolutions of Earth.
Apollo 10	Stafford, Young, Cernan	May 18–26, 1969	192.1	First LM orbit of Moon; call signs 'Charlie Brown' and 'Snoopy'; 31 revolutions of Moon (4 revolutions by undocked LM).
Apollo 11	Armstrong, Collins, Aldrin	July 16–24, 1969	195.3	First lunar landing; call signs 'Columbia' and 'Eagle'; lunar stay time 21 hours 36 minutes 21 seconds; Armstrong and Aldrin EVA (hatch open to hatch close) 2 hours 31 minutes 40 seconds; lunar surface samples 22 kg (49 lb); 30 revolutions of Moon.
Apollo 12	Conrad, Gordon, Bean	Nov. 14–24, 1969	244.6	'Yankee Clipper' and 'Intrepid'; stay time 31.5 hours; Conrad and Bean EVAs 3.9 and 3.8 hours; lunar samples 33.9 kg (74.7 lb) plus parts retrieved from nearby Surveyor 3 unmanned spacecraft; 45 revolutions of Moon.
Apollo 13	Lovell, Swigert, Haise	Apr. 11–17, 1970	142.9	'Odyssey' and 'Aquarius'; mission aborted after Service Module oxygen tank ruptured; using LM's oxygen and power until just before re-entry, crew returned safely to Earth.
Apollo 14	Shepard, Roosa, Mitchell	Jan. 31–Feb. 9, 1971	216.0	'Kitty Hawk' and 'Antares'; stay time 33.5 hours; Shepard and Mitchell EVAs 4.8 and 4.6 hours; samples 44 kg (97 lb); 34 revolutions of Moon.
Apollo 15	Scott, Worden, Irwin	July 26–Aug. 7, 1971	295.2	'Endeavour' and 'Falcon'; first use of lunar roving vehicle (Moon buggy); stay time 66.9 hours; Scott and Irwin EVAs 6.5, 7.2, and 4.8 hours: Worden trans-Earth EVA 38 minutes; samples 77 kg (170 lb); 74 revolutions of Moon.
Apollo 16	Young, Mattingly, Duke	April 16–27, 1972	265.9	'Casper' and 'Orion'; stay time 71 hours; Young and Duke EVAs 7.2, 7.4, and 5.7 hours; Mattingly trans-Earth EVA 1.4 hours; samples 97 kg (214 lb); 64 revolutions of Moon.
Apollo 17	Cernan, Evans, Schmitt	Dec. 7–19, 1972	301.9	'America' and 'Challenger'; stay time 75 hours; Cernan and Schmitt EVAs 7.2, 7.6, and 7.3 hours; Evans trans-Earth EVA 1 hour; samples 110 kg (243 lb); 75 revs of Moon.

Race for the Moon 15

Landing on Another World

There will never be moments like them again. A fragile metal contraption containing two Earthmen is gingerly descending to the surface of another world—the Moon. The date is July 20, 1969. The contraption is 'Eagle', the Lunar Module of the Apollo 11 spacecraft. The astronauts are Neil Armstrong and Edwin Aldrin, from the United States. Back on Earth at the Mission Control Center at Houston, Texas, the time is just after 4 o'clock in the afternoon. The spokesman at Houston is 'talking down' the Lunar Module with the astronauts, with occasional comments by Apollo Control.

As Eagle swooped ever nearer to the lunar surface, the tension became electrifying. Hundreds of millions of people, eavesdropping on the dialogue between Earth and Moon, held their breath. Was it to be triumph or disaster?

HOUSTON: Eagle, you're looking great, coming up 9 minutes.
CONTROL: We're now in the approach phase, looking good. Altitude 5,200 feet.
EAGLE: Manual auto attitude control is good.
CONTROL: Altitude 4,200.
HOUSTON: You're go for landing.
EAGLE: Roger, understand. Go for landing. 3,000 feet.
EAGLE: 12 alarm. 1201.
HOUSTON: Roger, 1201 alarm.
EAGLE: We're go. Hang tight. We're go. 2,000 feet. 47 degrees.
HOUSTON: Eagle looking great. You're go.
CONTROL: Altitude 1,600 . . . 1,400 feet.
EAGLE: 35 degrees. 35 degrees. 750, coming down at 23. 700 feet, 21 down. 33 degrees. 600 feet, down at 19 . . . 540 feet . . . 400 . . . 350 down at 4. . . . We're

pegged on horizontal velocity. 300 feet, down $3\frac{1}{2}$ . . . a minute. Got the shadow out there . . . altitude-velocity lights. $3\frac{1}{2}$ down, 220 feet. 13 forward. 11 forward, coming down nicely . . . 75 feet, things looking good.
HOUSTON: 60 seconds.
EAGLE: Lights on. Down $2\frac{1}{2}$. Forward. Forward. Good. 40 feet, down $2\frac{1}{2}$. Picking up some dust. 30 feet, $2\frac{1}{2}$ down. Faint shadow. 4 forward. Drifting to the right a little.
HOUSTON: 30 seconds.
EAGLE: Drifting right. Contact light. Okay, engine stop.
HOUSTON: We copy you down, Eagle.
EAGLE: Houston, Tranquillity Base here. The Eagle has landed.
HOUSTON: Roger, Tranquillity, we copy you on the ground. You got a bunch of guys about to turn blue. We're breathing again. Thanks a lot.

HERE MEN FROM THE PLANET EARTH FIRST SET FOOT UPON THE MOON JULY 1969, A. D.

WE CAME IN PEACE FOR ALL MANKIND

NEIL A. ARMSTRONG
ASTRONAUT

MICHAEL COLLINS
ASTRONAUT

EDWIN E. ALDRIN, JR.
ASTRONAUT

RICHARD NIXON
PRESIDENT, UNITED STATES OF AMERICA